WALKING FOR FITNESS

About the Authors

Lon H. Seiger. Dr. Seiger is an Assistant Professor of Health Education at Delta State University in Cleveland, Mississippi. An avid fitness walker, he has taught numerous fitness walking classes, presented several fitness walking programs throughout the country, and authored a chapter entitled "Fitness Walking" in another textbook. Dr. Seiger is a founder and faculty advisor for the Delta Road Scholars Club, an organization that promotes walking as an excellent activity for health and fitness. He holds a B.S. degree (in Health and Physical Education) from Southeastern Oklahoma State University, an M.Ed. (in Physical Education) from East Central Oklahoma State University, and an Ed.D. (in Health Education) from Oklahoma State University. Some of the organizations Dr. Seiger is active in include the American Alliance for Health, Physical Education, Recreation, and Dance; and the American School Health Association.

   James L. Hesson. Dr. Hesson is a professor at Delta State University in Cleveland, Mississippi. He has been recognized for excellence in teaching at the elementary, junior high, high school, and university levels in Nebraska, Utah, Texas, Mississippi, and Australia. For ten years Dr. Hesson coached championship men's gymnastics teams at the junior high school, high school, and university levels. He completed his doctoral degree as the valedictorian of his class at Brigham Young University. Dr. Hesson is the author of many articles as well as the author, coauthor, or contributing author of five books. He is a member of the American College of Sports Medicine; the American Alliance of Health, Physical Education, Recreation, and Dance; the National Strength and Conditioning Association; Phi Delta Kappa; and the Honor Society of Phi Kappa Phi.

To those who have made the greatest impact on my life: to Melissa, my lovely wife, for her love, support, and patience; to Mom, Dad, Jodi, Radd, and Darin, for their love, encouragement, and friendship; to Barry, Sharon, Bea, Diana, and Nancy, for their encouragement; and to my students, who are an endless source of sunshine and inspiration.

Lon H. Seiger

To Margie, Jennifer, and David, for their patience, support, and love; to all my students who have taught me how to help them learn; and to the greatest teacher of all, who is with us every step of the way.

James L. Hesson

WALKING FOR FITNESS

Lon H. Seiger
Assistant Professor, Delta State University

James Hesson
Professor, Delta State University

 Wm. C. Brown Publishers

Book Team

Editor *Chris Rogers*
Developmental Editors *Sue Pulvermacher-Alt/Cindy Kuhrasch*
Production Coordinator *Kay Driscoll*

WCB **Wm. C. Brown Publishers**

President *G. Franklin Lewis*
Vice President, Editor-in-Chief *George Wm. Bergquist*
Vice President, Director of Production *Beverly Kolz*
Vice President, National Sales Manager *Bob McLaughlin*
Director of Marketing *Thomas E. Doran*
Marketing Communications Manager *Edward Bartell*
Marketing Manager *Kathy Law Laube*
Production Editorial Manager *Colleen A. Yonda*
Production Editorial Manager *Julie A. Kennedy*
Publishing Services Manager *Karen J. Slaght*
Manager of Visuals and Design *Faye M. Schilling*

Consulting Editor
Physical Education
Aileene Lockhart
Texas Women's University

Sports and Fitness Series Evaluation Materials Editor
Jane A. Mott
Texas Women's University

Cover design by Jeanne Marie Regan

Printed in the United States of America by Wm. C. Brown Publishers,
2460 Kerper Boulevard, Dubuque, IA 52001

10 9 8 7 6 5

Contents

Preface

This text has been developed to assist walkers of any age, sex, background, and skill level to acquire the knowledge, skills, and attitudes necessary for participation in a lifelong fitness walking program. Designed primarily for an introductory course at the college level, the text can also be used in a variety of other settings.

The material is presented in a style that is easy to understand for the beginning fitness walker. However, intermediate and advanced levels of knowledge and skill can be achieved when the material is thoroughly mastered.

This is not intended to be a total fitness book. The focus of *Walking for Fitness* is on the components of health-related physical fitness that are of greatest concern in our society—cardiovascular fitness and body composition.

Activities are presented throughout the text to provide meaningful learning experiences. Other special features include a walking test, three different walking programs, and guidelines for effective exercise.

The first chapter provides a brief overview of the popularity of walking. Chapter 2 outlines the benefits of fitness walking. Chapter 3 describes clothing and equipment, and chapter 4 details safety considerations. Guidelines for warm-up, cool down, and flexibility are explained in chapter 5.

Chapter 6 describes the Rockport Fitness Walking Test. Chapter 7 illustrates fitness walking programs recommended by Rockport and the American Heart Association. In addition, guidelines for effective exercise are presented for those who prefer to develop their own fitness walking programs. Specific fitness walking techniques are presented in chapter 8.

The recommendations for weight loss in chapter 9 and the mental benefits of walking, as described in chapter 10, are important to many walkers.

Chapter 11 provides motivational strategies for sticking with a fitness walking program. Chapter 12 explains that fitness walking is only one part of a larger total health program.

We believe you will enjoy reading *Walking for Fitness* and find the information in it useful. Each day we make choices that either enhance or detract from our health. Fitness walking is a positive choice that can make a significant contribution to a healthy life-style.

Acknowledgments

The authors wish to extend their appreciation to Clement Jee for his excellent work on the cover photo and for the majority of the photography throughout the book; Bill Powell for his photographic contributions; Judge Little's Sporting Goods of Cleveland, Mississippi for providing the warm-up suits used for the cover photo; Lori Atkins, Kippy Betts, Scott Brooks, Laurita Koll, Maria Lee, and Karen Williams for their time and patience as models; and Dr. Milton Wilder, Dr. Lisso Simmons, Dr. Frank McArthur, and Dr. Kent Wyatt for the supportive academic climate they have created at Delta State University.

The Walking Boom

1

Millions of Americans have turned walking into the number one fitness activity in the United States. Over 55 million Americans have already chosen walking as their favorite exercise. Experts predict that this number will soon increase to over 100 million.

Walking is one of the safest and most effective forms of exercise to improve health and develop physical fitness. Doctors are recommending walking as the best exercise for many Americans.

What Is Fitness Walking?

Fitness walking refers to the type of walking that produces health and fitness benefits. For walking to be considered fitness walking, it must be done fast enough, long enough, and often enough to produce desirable health benefits. In addition, the walker must use correct walking techniques.

More and more Americans are walking to improve their health and fitness.

A walking event sponsored by the American Cancer Society.

Are There Organized Walking Events?

There are over 10,000 walking events held every year, and this number is increasing. In the striding events, participants walk a six-mile course in paradelike fashion. Many of the traditional running events are now encouraging walkers to enter. There has also been an increase in the number of racewalking events.

Are There Walking Clubs?

Walking clubs are being formed all over the country. Over 6,500 clubs are registered with *The Walking Magazine*. The Walkers and Talkers and The Road Scholars are two clubs that have turned fitness walking into an enjoyable social event. Why not form a walking club in your area? It's a healthy way to spend time with friends.

Many persons enjoy walking with a group. How can you locate walking clubs in your area? Try calling the Recreation or Physical Education Department at a university, the municipal recreation department, or a local mall office.

Mall walking has become popular as a safe, climate-controlled fitness activity.

What Is Mall Walking?

At many indoor shopping malls throughout the United States, walkers are allowed to exercise before the stores open. This has provided many walkers with a comfortable and dependable place to exercise all year. Mall walking offers the additional attractions of personal safety and group participation.

Are There Fitness Walking Shoes?

The shoe industry provides further evidence of the growing popularity of fitness walking. A few years ago it was difficult to find a good pair of walking shoes, but now there are over forty companies making them. Some companies are taking the design features of their fitness walking shoes and including them in dress shoes. It is now possible to wear comfortable shoes all day, not just when you exercise.

Where Can I Obtain Fitness Walking Information?

In recent years there has been an increase in the amount of fitness walking information available. This information has appeared in magazines, books, brochures, on television, radio, video, and audio cassettes.

Is Fitness Walking Really an "Ideal" Exercise?

Why all of this interest in a form of exercise as old as the human race in an age of high-tech exercise machines? There may be as many reasons for this interest as there are fitness walkers. However, most people are interested in fitness walking because it is an enjoyable way to improve their health.

Fitness walking can be an escape from the high-tech life-style. It requires no machines, videos, or expensive club memberships. No one is excluded from fitness walking because of age, body type, or skill level. It can be done almost anywhere and at almost anytime.

Fitness walking is a versatile exercise. It can be started on a small scale and increased as conditioning improves. The techniques are not difficult to learn, and there are several variations of walking to choose from: strolling, everyday walking, hiking, backpacking, snowshoeing, stairwalking, brisk walking, and racewalking. You may think of other variations. These variations allow you to find the best workout for your age, interest, and fitness level.

For all these reasons, and many others, health professionals are recommending fitness walking as an excellent form of exercise.

Why has participation in fitness walking increased so dramatically during the past few years?

Can Walking Improve Physical Fitness?

For years it was thought that walking would not provide enough exercise to produce any cardiovascular benefit. The results of scientific research have proven that fitness walkers are able to reach the training heart rates necessary to produce an improvement in cardiovascular fitness.

Using correct walking techniques, with accelerated arm and leg movements, fitness walkers use most of the muscles in their bodies. Brisk walking produces an increased oxygen demand. This increased demand for oxygen makes the circulatory and respiratory systems work harder than normal, which improves the functioning of the heart and lungs.

Isn't Walking Slow and Boring?

Walking can be fast and interesting. Walking speeds may vary from a slow shuffle of less than one mile per hour to racewalking at speeds in excess of ten miles per hour. World-class racewalkers can walk a mile in under six minutes and maintain that speed for more than twelve miles. Most people could not even run one six-minute mile, much less maintain that speed for twelve miles.

Fitness walkers generally walk a mile in about twelve to seventeen minutes. Using proper form, with accelerated arm and leg swings, speed can be dramatically increased.

Walking speed varies greatly depending on the type of walking and the individual. Approximately how quickly do fitness walkers cover a mile? How does this compare with the speed of world-class racewalkers?

When approached with a positive attitude, walking is not boring. There are many interesting things you can do while you walk—for example, listening to a tape to learn something new, listening to your favorite music or to the news, talking with friends, releasing stress, solving personal problems, exploring new areas, appreciating nature, praying, and meditating.

Isn't Walking Only for the Elderly and Injured?

It is true that fitness walking is an excellent exercise for older people, for cardiac patients, and for those who have been injured. However, walking is not limited to these people. Fitness walking is a safe and effective form of exercise that has also attracted young, healthy individuals who want to become more fit.

Who Is Robert Sweetgall?

Some of the increased awareness of and interest in fitness walking may be traced to Robert Sweetgall. Within one year, Sweetgall lost several family members to heart disease, the leading cause of death in the United States. The losses encouraged him to change his life-style and communicate to Americans the importance of fitness. After a year of training and planning, Robert set out to complete the "50/50: Walk for the Health of It." His mission was to walk through all fifty states in fifty weeks to demonstrate and communicate the value of fitness walking for cardiovascular health. His walk across America reached millions of people with the message that fitness walking is an exercise almost anyone can do to keep healthy.

The United States is experiencing a walking boom. You have probably noticed the increased number of people in your community who are walking to improve their health and fitness. Why not choose to do something positive about your own health and fitness? Join the fitness walking movement.

Activity 1a

The purpose of this activity is to observe the popularity of fitness walking.

Early in the morning, before most people go to work, or in the evening, after most people return home from work, see how many people you can observe walking for exercise. Look in your neighborhood, local parks, outdoor tracks, and other likely places.

Count and record the number of people you see walking for exercise during a thirty-minute period of time.

Robert Sweetgall, who walked across America to promote fitness walking.

Benefits of Fitness Walking

2

Why Exercise?

Of the ten leading causes of death in the United States, nine are related to life-style (see table 2.1). One of these harmful lifestyle behaviors is sedentary living. If you live a sedentary life-style, you can expect a premature decline in your body's ability to function. If this deterioration is allowed to continue, eventually one of your organ systems will not be able to perform its life-sustaining function and you will experience a life-threatening illness, or even death.

Long before death occurs, however, you may suffer through years of "not feeling very good." Nothing definite, no specific symptoms, just the overall feeling that something isn't quite right. The feeling that life is difficult rather than enjoyable. The feeling that it is about all you can do to plow through another day. These are feelings frequently expressed by people in poor physical condition.

The good news is that a moderate amount of exercise on a regular basis will improve the functioning of your body. Exercise can help you look better, feel

Table 2.1   The Ten Leading Causes of Death in the United States for All Ages.

Rank	Cause
1	Heart Disease
2	Cancer
3	Stroke
4	Accidents
5	Chronic Lung Disease
6	Pneumonia and Influenza
7	Diabetes
8	Suicide
9	Cirrhosis of the Liver
10	Atherosclerosis

Source: National Center for Health Statistics, United States Department of Health and Human Services.

better, and enjoy life. It is difficult to express how good life can be when you are in excellent health and excellent physical condition. Those who have experienced optimal health usually continue to choose positive lifestyle behaviors.

Why Aerobic Exercise?

You are an aerobic organism. The term *aerobic* (a-rōw'-bik) refers to life forms that require oxygen. In recent years it has also been used to identify exercise that requires you to use large amounts of oxygen. You could live for weeks without food, for days without water, but only about five to ten minutes without oxygen. How well your body operates depends upon your ability to get oxygen to every living cell.

Oxygen enters your body with the air you breathe into your lungs. Approximately one-fifth of normal, unpolluted air is oxygen. Some of the oxygen that enters your lungs is transferred into your blood. Your heart then pumps the oxygenated blood to all of your cells.

Any behavior that reduces the functioning of your respiratory or circulatory systems also reduces your ability to transport life-sustaining oxygen to your cells. Sedentary living reduces your ability to deliver oxygen to all parts of your body. This decline in oxygen delivery could be considered a slow form of suffocation; no wonder it results in "not feeling very good." If this deterioration continues, eventually you will only be able to take in enough oxygen to sustain your life in a resting state.

A poorly conditioned person may experience a sudden demand for increased oxygen delivery. Since their body is not capable of delivering more oxygen to the heart muscle, which is now working harder than normal, some of the oxygen-starved heart muscle tissue may die. The affected cardiac muscle tissue can then no longer contract, and the heart may not be able to continue to pump oxygenated blood to any of the other living body cells. This is a simplified explanation of one type of heart attack. Of course, without a continuous supply of life-sustaining oxygen, the other cells of the body cannot survive either.

Humans are aerobic organisms. Therefore, exercises that improve one's ability to obtain and use oxygen are the most beneficial. These exercises, which stimulate the development of the oxygen delivery system, are called aerobic exercises. Aerobic exercises typically use large muscle groups in a rhythmic and continuous manner. Table 2.2 lists some of the benefits of aerobic exercise.

(a)

(b)

(c)

(d)

(e)

(f)

Six major aerobic activities: (a) walking, (b) swimming, (c) aerobic dancing, (d) water aerobics, (e) bicycling, and (f) jogging.

Table 2.2   Benefits of Aerobic Exercise.

The following benefits have been reported as a result of a moderate amount of aerobic exercise performed on a regular basis. While all of these benefits are still under investigation, some have been studied more thoroughly than others. Biological adaptation to exercise is a gradual process that requires consistent, long-term participation.

Heart

—Increased strength of the heart muscle
—Increased stroke volume
—Increased cardiac output
—Increased heart volume
—Decreased resting heart rate
—Decreased exercise heart rate at a standard work load
—Decreased risk of cardiovascular disease
—Decreased risk of heart attack
—Decreased severity of heart attack if one does occur
—Increased chance of surviving a heart attack if one does occur

Blood

—Increased blood flow
—Increased total blood volume
—Increased number of red blood cells
—Increased oxygen-carrying capacity of the blood
—Increased high-density lipoproteins
—Increased ability to extract oxygen from the blood
—Decrease in harmful blood fats

Blood Vessels

—Increased capillary size
—Increased number of open capillaries
—Increased peripheral circulation
—Increased coronary circulation
—Decreased resting blood pressure for some individuals
—Decreased risk of atherosclerosis

Lungs

—Increased minute volume of air
—Increased rate of breathing during exercise
—Increased volume per breath during exercise

Body Fat

—Decrease in total body fat
—Decrease in percentage of body fat
—Maintenance of healthy body-fat level
—Decreased appetite if exercise is performed just before a meal
—Decrease in total body weight

Muscle

—Increased lean body weight
—Increased muscle tissue
—Increased muscle strength
—Increased muscle endurance

Bone

—Increased bone density
—Increased bone strength
—Increased joint strength
—Decreased risk of osteoporosis

Table 2.2   (continued)

Connective Tissue

—Increased tendon strength
—Increased ligament strength
—Increased joint strength

Endurance

—Increased work efficiency
—Increased sports performance
—Increased ability to use oxygen
—Increased physical ability to meet emergency situations
—Increased ease of recovery after hard work
—Increased cardiovascular endurance
—Increased functioning of oxygen-supply organ systems

Resistance to Disease

—Increased resistance to disease
—Increased general health

Appearance

—Improved appearance
—Improved posture
—Decreased waistline

Stress

—Decrease in emotional stress

Mental

—Improved self-concept
—Increase in positive attitudes and feelings
—Increased self-confidence
—Increased self-discipline
—Increased independence for many older citizens
—Decrease tendency toward depression
—Improved soundness of sleep
—Decrease in mental tension
—Increased social interaction with healthy people
—Increased resistance to fatigue
—Increased feeling of success
—Increased enjoyment of leisure time
—Increased enjoyment of work
—Increased quality of life
—Increased sense of well-being

Why Fitness Walking?

Fitness walking is an excellent aerobic exercise for many reasons.

Lifetime Exercise

Walking is an exercise that you can participate in for most of your life. To obtain the greatest benefit from exercise, it must be consistent and lifelong—something you can participate in twelve months a year, every year, and not just seasonally.

Walking is a lifetime exercise.

Walking is the preferred exercise of many adults. Unlike some team sports, walking is an exercise you can perform for the rest of your life.

Everyone Can Participate

Walking has few restrictions. Almost everyone can participate in fitness walking. No special sports skills are necessary to achieve a beneficial amount of exercise.

If you are overweight, walking is ideal because it puts less strain on your bones and joints than other aerobic activities.

Posture

Fitness walking promotes good posture by strengthening many of your muscles. Good posture allows you to function more effectively, expending a minimal amount of energy. People with good posture experience less strain in their muscles, tendons, ligaments, and joints. Good posture also conveys an impression of alertness, confidence, and attractiveness.

Cardiac Rehabilitation

Walking is the primary exercise in many cardiac rehabilitation programs. It is a good exercise for those recovering from heart attacks because walking is an exercise that cardiac patients are familiar with, are not afraid of, can continue for

All body types can participate in fitness walking.

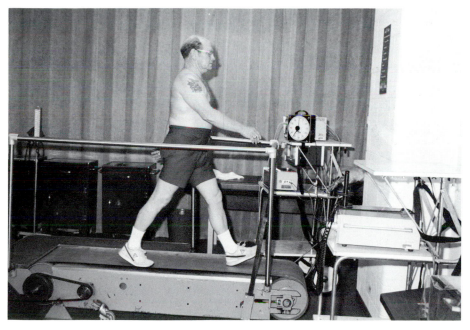

Walking is an ideal exercise for cardiac rehabilitation patients.

An injured football player walks to aid the recovery process.

the rest of their lives, can easily monitor, can start at a low level, and can progressively increase. Walking helps the heart attack victims get on their feet again. It helps them regain some control over their lives and feel optimistic about their futures.

Recovery from Injury

Walking can be an excellent exercise when you are recovering from injuries, especially leg injuries. When muscles are not used, they atrophy (decrease in size and strength). Walking is an ideal exercise in the recovery process because it helps to rebuild muscle tissue.

Safe and Natural Exercise

Many former joggers have decided to participate in fitness walking. The force of landing on each foot during jogging is about 3½ to 4 times your body weight, while the force of landing on each foot during walking is about 1 to 1½ times your body weight. Therefore, joint and muscle injuries are less likely to occur with a walking program.

Walking produces balanced leg muscle development and is one of the most natural exercises for the human body. Your body was designed for movement, not inactivity.

An Inexpensive Activity

Fitness walking does not require expensive facilities, equipment, or club membership. Of course, as fitness walking continues its rapid growth in popularity, creative people will develop innovative products, facilities, clothing, equipment, and memberships that will find a market. If you enjoy these new products and services and can afford them, that's fine—just remember that they are not necessary for you to gain benefits from fitness walking.

Improved Fitness for Sports

You can start slowly with fitness walking and gradually build to a high level of fitness. For people who have not been exercising, walking is recommended as a starter program to prepare for other sports.

Walking is also a component of interval training programs for highly trained athletes. Interval training alternates work intervals of intense exercise with recovery intervals of less intense exercise. An example of interval training is sprinting during work intervals and walking during recovery intervals.

Easier to Stick With

The dropout rate for fitness walking is lower than for many other exercise programs. Walking is convenient and accessible. It can be used as a form of transportation. Walking can be combined with other enjoyable activities such as

Walking is a convenient and enjoyable method of transportation.

Family and friends can enjoy walking together.

sightseeing or carrying on a conversation. Since walking can be more enjoyable than some of the other fitness activities, you are more likely to stick with a walking program.

Social Activity

Walking is an excellent family or group activity. It can be a social and fitness activity at the same time. Joggers often find it difficult to maintain a conversation as they exercise. Walkers are more able to maintain a conversation due to the lower intensity and longer duration of many walking programs.

Walking provides an excellent opportunity for family members and friends to spend regular time together. It provides a time to discuss personal and family needs, wants, goals, and dreams.

Instead of going out for a drink or dessert, why not go for a walk?

Weight Loss

Fitness walking is an excellent way to lose weight. Since many people are interested in losing excess body fat, an entire chapter in this text is devoted to this important benefit of fitness walking.

Appreciating the Outdoors

One of the advantages of walking is that it provides an opportunity to be outdoors. Many people in the United States spend the majority of their time indoors. Fitness walking is a good way to explore your surroundings and discover the natural beauty around you. Hiking and backpacking are popular forms of walking.

Walking gives you the opportunity to enjoy nature.

Exercise During Pregnancy

Walking is one of the safest and best exercises during pregnancy. Many pregnant women make the mistake of avoiding all physical activity and become totally deconditioned for the most demanding physical activity of their lives. When they do finally give birth, they are often in their weakest and poorest physical condition as a result of nine months of deconditioning. Adequate exercise and good nutrition bring many benefits to the developing child as well as the mother.

Fitness walking is a good exercise for pregnant women because it is a low-impact activity. Also, the intensity level can be easily monitored and adjusted to the fairly rapid biological changes that occur during pregnancy.

Fits into a Daily Routine

You may choose to walk at a time that best fits your schedule. Some people prefer to walk early in the morning to start the day. Others prefer to walk late at night, still others choose to walk at noon or during breaks. These are only a few of the ways people fit walking into their daily routines.

Walking is an excellent exercise during pregnancy.

(a)

(b)

Walking can fit into anyone's daily routine.

Activity 2a

The purpose of this activity is to determine why you want to participate in a fitness walking program.

On a blank sheet of paper, list the benefits you would like to receive from your fitness walking program. Don't evaluate them at this time; just list them as quickly as you can think of them. When you can't think of any more, go back and place a check next to the top three benefits you hope to achieve. Of those three, which one is the most important to you? Why?

Clothing and Equipment

3

One of the advantages of fitness walking is that you don't need to spend much money on special clothing and equipment. Some activities, such as skiing and scuba diving, require expensive equipment that might only be used a few times a year. Most fitness walking clothing and equipment is relatively inexpensive and can be used every day.

The most important piece of clothing or equipment you can buy for fitness walking is a good pair of walking shoes.

Walking Shoes

Approximately 87 percent of all Americans have suffered from some type of foot problem. Many foot problems are caused by wearing shoes that do not fit properly, or shoes that are worn out. When shopping for shoes, it is wise to spend a little extra time and money to get good quality and a proper fit. After all, you can't buy a new pair of feet.

When shopping for fitness walking shoes be sure to allow enough time. Be a good comparison shopper. Try on at least three different brands and as many styles as possible. Even if a shoe is ranked as the best or the most popular style, it may not fit you as comfortably as another brand or model.

Walking shoes should feel comfortable when you first try them on. There is very little "break in" necessary for good quality walking shoes. Be wary of the salesperson who tells you an uncomfortable pair of walking shoes will feel fine after you break them in.

When you try on walking shoes, test them on a hard surface rather than the padded carpet commonly found in shoe stores. This test will help you determine the amount of cushion and comfort the shoes provide.

Outer Sole

The outer sole is the material on the bottom of a shoe. It should be made from a durable material. A good walking shoe has a rocker-shaped sole. Like a good rocking chair, this helps your foot rock forward from heel to toe.

Walking shoes usually have a tread design for traction. However, it is not as deep as is commonly found on running shoes.

Some people experience eversion when they walk or run. *Eversion* is the anatomical term for a movement in which the bottom of the foot turns outward. Commercially, the term *pronation* is being used and has gained popular acceptance to describe this foot movement. Pronation is actually an anatomical term describing a forearm movement.

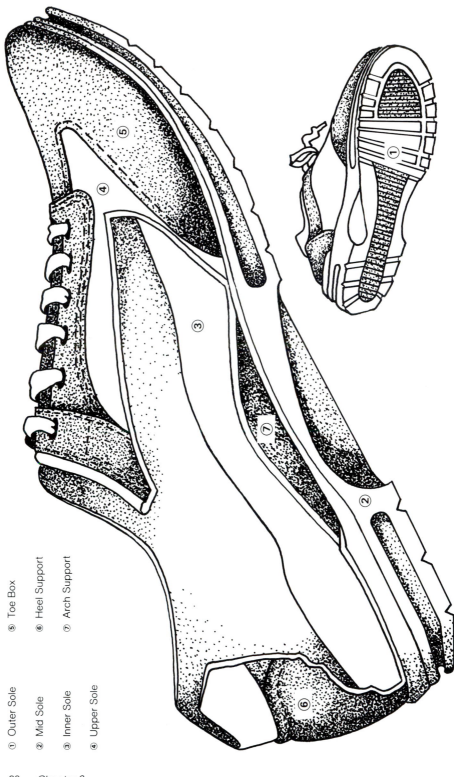

① Outer Sole　　⑤ Toe Box

② Mid Sole　　　⑥ Heel Support

③ Inner Sole　　⑦ Arch Support

④ Upper Sole

Important components of a good quality walking shoe.

A shoe with antipronation construction is designed to keep the sole of your foot from turning too far outward. If excessive eversion (pronation) occurs with every step you take, extensive jogging or walking could eventually cause injury. Therefore, some of the better running and walking shoes feature antipronation construction for those who need the extra support.

Midsole

The midsole is a cushioning layer between the outer and inner soles. Since the primary purpose of the midsole is to absorb shock, it can be made from a variety of materials and has been designed in many different ways.

Unfortunately, there is no exact way for most people to determine when the midsole has lost its ability to absorb shock. The outer sole and upper part of the shoe may look fine, but if the midsole has lost its resiliency, it is time to get a new pair of walking shoes.

Inner Sole

The inner sole makes direct contact with your foot. This sole should include an arch support and a heel cup. Some shoes have an arch support that can be added to, or removed from, the inner sole. The inner sole may also provide additional air or gel cushioning.

The inner sole can be removed from many good quality walking shoes. One advantage of this is that you can air out the inner sole after a workout. A second advantage is that the inner sole can be replaced if it wears out. And a third advantage is that a podiatrist or orthopedic doctor can make an inner sole that perfectly fits your foot.

What are the advantages of a walking shoe with a removable inner sole?

Upper Shoe

The upper shoe is often made of leather because it is a durable, supple material. The toe-box portion of the shoe should be wide enough that the front part of the foot can spread. This will allow you to push off with all your toes.

The heel of the upper shoe should include a stiff material to support and hold the foot in position. Good walking shoes are notched at the top of the heel support to minimize irritation of the Achilles tendon.

Some walking shoes feature reflective material as a safety measure for those who walk in the dark.

Size and Comfort

One of your feet may be longer than the other. Try on both shoes. Purchase shoes that are comfortable for the longer foot. You may need to wear an extra sock on the smaller foot if there is a great difference.

It's a good idea to try shoes on before you buy them. You may find that different brands of shoes fit differently, even if the size marked on the shoes is the same. Also, the size of your feet may change over time.

If you choose to buy your walking shoes through a mail order company, make sure the company has a return policy in case the shoes you order don't fit.

Walking shoes do not require much of a "break-in" period. However, it's still a good idea to alternate your old shoes with your new shoes for a couple of weeks. This allows your feet to gradually adjust to the change.

Walking shoes should fit comfortably, and not be too tight or too loose. They should extend at least one-fourth of an inch beyond your big toe. Your feet should not feel squeezed into a narrow shoe. You may find some variation in the size of walking shoes depending on the manufacturer.

Do not sacrifice comfort for name brand, style, or sale price. It is important that your walking shoes be comfortable. Your walking shoes should not hurt your feet.

Shoe Flexibility

All three soles and the upper shoe should bend at the ball of your foot. A good walking shoe should not be stiff at this point.

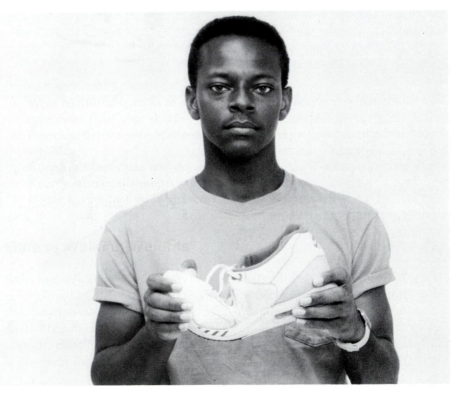

A good walking shoe is flexible.

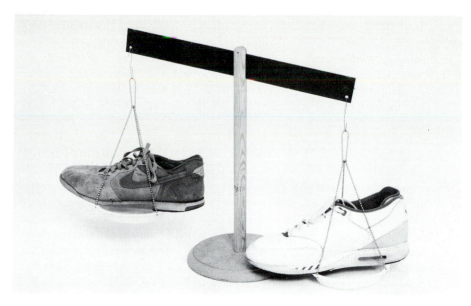

Fitness walking shoes vary in weight.

Weight

Racewalking shoes are lighter than training shoes. A few ounces of additional weight may make a difference in a race. However, most fitness walkers prefer training shoes, which are more durable.

Quality

Look carefully at walking shoes you are considering buying. Is the shoe made from quality materials? Is the shoe well-constructed? Is the stitching carefully done? Is the upper shoe securely fastened to the midsole?

Fitness walking shoes are an investment in your health. Make a good investment. Insist on quality.

Activity 3a

The purpose of this activity is to investigate different types of walking shoes.

Visit a store that carries walking shoes. Observe the shoes carefully to evaluate its components. Which shoes seem to possess the better quality parts? Which shoes are the cheapest? Which are the most expensive?

You may want to feel the differences among walking shoes by trying on different brands. Which shoes offer the most support? Which shoes feel comfortable? Which offer the most cushion? Which provide the most stability?

If you are serious about walking for your health and fitness, make a wise investment and purchase good quality walking shoes. Your feet will be glad you did.

Clothing

Fitness walking clothes should be lightweight and allow freedom of movement.

Cotton socks are excellent for absorbing moisture. For extra comfort you may want to put on an extra pair of socks. Another option would be to buy socks containing extra cushioning in the heel and forefoot areas. This extra cushioning may reduce friction and help prevent blisters.

A sports bra for women and an athletic supporter for men will provide firm support and make fitness walking more comfortable.

Hot Weather Clothing

Clothes that are light colored and loose fitting are cooler during hot weather. Light-colored clothing reflects some of the suns rays and loose-fitting clothing allows air to circulate next to your skin.

Walking shorts should allow free and easy movement. Lightweight shorts with built in briefs add support with little increase in bulk. Shorts made of thick material might have bulky inseams that rub the insides of your thighs.

Another advantage of lightweight shorts is that they dry quickly. It is possible to rinse them out after each workout and have them clean and dry for the next day.

Shirts that are loose fitting and made of natural fabrics, such as cotton, absorb perspiration and allow air to move next to your skin.

A good hot-weather walking hat should include a raised, vented crown to allow air to circulate between the top of the hat and your head. In sunny weather the brim of the hat should protect your eyes and forehead from the harmful rays of the sun. On hot, sunny days a hat helps prevent headaches and fatigue.

Cold Weather Clothing

For fitness walking in cold weather, dress in layers of clothing. This will allow you to remove layers to regulate your body temperature as you walk. Keeping warm while exercising in cold weather is not as much of a problem as you might think. Approximately 75 percent of the energy released during muscle contraction is in the form of heat energy. Therefore, your muscles produce a lot of heat during exercise. You can use your layers of clothing to control the amount of heat next to your skin.

The innermost layer of clothing should be made of a material that will keep you warm and dry. It should draw moisture away from your skin because it is difficult to stay warm if you're wet. This layer should be made of a loosely woven fabric with air spaces that hold warm air next to your skin.

The next layer on your upper body might be a long sleeved T-shirt or turtleneck. On top of that, add a wool pullover or a sweatshirt.

The top layer could be a cotton sweatsuit or a synthetic fabric depending upon the weather conditions. If the weather is wet, the outer layer should be waterproof. If the weather is cold and windy, the outer layer serves as a windbreaker.

(a)　　　　　　　　　　　　　　　　　　(b)

(a) Hot and (b) cold weather clothing suitable for fitness walking.

Warm-up suits with air vents enhance evaporation. This reduces the amount of moisture inside the suit. These warm-up suits hold heat in while allowing moisture to escape.

A knit hat is recommended for cold weather. Wool is a popular material for warm knit hats. A hat or hood helps to hold in body heat. As much as two-thirds of your body heat can be lost if your head is not covered.

Gloves or mittens should be worn during fitness walking because the fingers are especially vulnerable to the cold. A woven material allows perspiration to draw away from the skin, while a solid synthetic material allows perspiration to accumulate inside. Natural fabrics, such as cotton or wool, work well.

Body Suits

Body suits made of lycra or lycra-blend material are available. These suits conform to the shape of your body but do not restrict movement.

Sauna Suits

Rubber suits or sauna suits are dangerous and should not be worn while fitness walking. These suits are made of nonporous materials. This means that air and moisture cannot pass through them. Sauna suits are also elasticized at the neck, wrists, waist, and ankles. During exercise, the air between the suit and your skin becomes hot and humid. It is possible to experience extreme heat and humidity inside the sauna suit even on a comfortable day. Extreme heat may lead to heat-related disorders such as heat cramps, heat exhaustion, and heat stroke.

Body suits.

A hazardous sauna suit.

Some people wear sauna suits during exercise so they will perspire more. They believe it is possible to "sweat off" body fat. Heavy sweating may result in a rapid but temporary weight loss. However, the pounds represent fluid loss, not fat loss. The fluid (and the weight) is quickly regained with any food or liquid intake. This is an unhealthy and ineffective way to attempt to lose weight. A healthy way is to expend more calories than you take in over a relatively long period of time.

Equipment

A few pieces of fitness walking equipment can make walking safer and more enjoyable.

Sunglasses

Sunglasses are essential to protect your eyes from the harmful direct rays of the sun and from reflected glare. The best sunglasses provide UV (ultraviolet) protection. You may experience dizziness and temporary vision impairment if your eyes are not shielded from direct sunlight.

Fitness walking equipment.

Reflective Material

Many people walk after dark. This is especially true during the winter months when the daylight hours are short. Reflective tape can be added to your walking clothes and shoes. Reflective vests are also available. If you decide not to use reflective material, at least wear light-colored clothing that can be seen more easily in the dark.

Pulsemeter

A pulsemeter allows you to monitor your heart rate while you are walking. You need to reach a prescribed exercise heart rate to receive an adequate training effect. A pulsemeter can inform you when you have reached your exercise heart rate. It provides feedback that can help you stay at the correct exercise heart rate for the duration of your walk.

Pedometer

A pedometer is a device that measures how far you walk. Usually it counts the number of steps you take. On some models you need to preset your approximate stride length.

Backpack

Backpacks are useful for one-day hikes and weekend trips. In your backpack you can carry first aid items, a change of socks, and extra layers of clothing. Waist-packs are also available.

Hand Weights

Hand weights may be carried during fitness walking to increase muscular effort, energy expenditure, oxygen demand, and heart rate. Beginners should not carry weights. The additional exercise load could be harmful for the unconditioned beginner. Hand weights are recommended for intermediate or advanced fitness walkers only.

Quality clothing and equipment can increase your fitness walking enjoyment. Consider which items are important to you and make use of them in your fitness walking program.

Safety

Know well

4

Fitness walking has many benefits. However, as with any activity that involves human movement, care must be taken to avoid injury. Knowing some of the possible dangers will enable you to walk safely.

Medical Clearance

You should get medical clearance from your physician before starting a fitness walking program.

Activity 4a

The purpose of this activity is to help you determine if you are medically ready to participate in a fitness walking program. Answer each of the following questions.

1. Are you over thirty-five years of age?
2. Do you have any type of cardiovascular disease?
3. Do you have high blood pressure?
4. Do you ever experience chest pain?
5. Do you ever experience breathlessness?
6. Do you have any bone or joint problems?
7. Do you ever feel faint or dizzy?
8. Do you smoke?
9. Have you been inactive for the last two years?
10. Do you have a weight problem?
11. Do you have any medical condition that could cause a problem if you started walking?

If you responded "yes" to any of these questions, or if you have any doubt about your health, get medical clearance from your physician before starting a fitness walking program.

Listen to Your Body

Each year, thousands of enthusiastic people, dedicated to new fitness goals, exercise too much the first day. This results in unnecessary pain and injury. When you begin an exercise program, start slowly.

The beneficial changes that occur in the human body as a result of an exercise program are best obtained with a slow start and gentle, steady progress.

It is common to experience some mild muscle soreness a day or two after beginning a new exercise program. However, two of the best methods of relieving mild muscle soreness are static stretch and aerobic exercise. These are both included in a good fitness walking workout. After a few workouts, your muscles will adapt to the new activity and the muscle soreness will diminish.

If you progress slowly into your new exercise program, you should not experience any extreme pain. Pain is generally an indication of injury. If you do experience extreme pain, you should stop exercising and seek medical attention. Learn to listen to your body for feedback about the effects of your fitness walking program.

Extreme Weather

One excuse many people use for not exercising on a regular basis is the weather. Fitness walking can be performed in a wide range of weather conditions. There are some dangers associated with exercising in extreme weather conditions. However, if you know the dangers and take precautions, the weather should rarely be an excuse for not exercising.

Hot Weather

The dangers of exercising in hot weather should be taken seriously. Loss of body fluid may impair performance. Excessive loss of body fluid may lead to heat cramps, heat exhaustion, or heat stroke. Those who are poorly conditioned, overweight, older, or not acclimatized to exercise in the heat are at higher risk. People who have previously suffered from heat disorders should be especially careful.

To reduce the risk of heat disorders, drink plenty of water about thirty minutes before walking. Continue to drink small amounts of water frequently during your workout. After exercising, drink as much water as you want. Some studies have indicated that it is impossible to drink too much water. While there are many sports drinks on the market, plain water is hard to beat as a replacement fluid. Besides being absorbed quickly, it is generally the most available and least expensive beverage.

Other hot weather precautions include wearing light-colored, loose-fitting clothing; walking during the coolest times of the day; reducing exercise intensity; and reducing exercise duration. Remember, the purpose of exercise is to improve your health, not endanger it.

Cold Weather

Dehydration can be a problem when exercising during cold weather. Your body loses fluids more quickly than you realize. Perspiration quickly evaporates when the air is dry. Even if you are not thirsty, drink plenty of water before and after cold-weather walking. Also, avoid diuretic liquids such as coffee and tea, since they cause more frequent urination.

Frostbite is a danger in cold weather, but with the proper precautions it can be avoided. With freezing temperatures and windy conditions, frostbite can occur within minutes on the most vulnerable parts of your body—your hands, nose, ears, and toes. Be sure that these body parts are well-covered with clothing during extremely cold weather. If you are walking during cold weather and notice any tissue that feels numb or is turning hard and white, take immediate action. Go indoors where the air temperature is warmer, and soak the tissue in warm water. Never use hot water because tissue damage may occur.

Hypothermia occurs when your body temperature becomes dangerously low. For survival, the temperature inside your body must remain fairly constant at all times. Prolonged exposure to the cold, accompanied by excessive loss of body heat, can lead to a life-threatening condition in which your core body temperature drops to a dangerous level. The symptoms of hypothermia include disorientation, sluggishness, slurred speech, and a stumbling gait. Be sure you dress warmly enough to maintain your core body temperature when walking during cold weather.

People with high blood pressure need to dress warmly because shivering elevates blood pressure. Angina (chest pain) can also be caused by exposure to the cold. If you have angina and the air temperature is low, cover your mouth and nose with a scarf while walking. If you have any kind of cardiovascular disease, you should walk indoors when the outdoor temperature drops below 20° F. Mall walking has become popular, especially in colder climates.

Since cold weather is often accompanied by snow and ice, the danger of slipping and falling is increased during winter weather. If you walk outside in the cold, it's a good idea to walk where other people are nearby to help in case you fall.

Some people mistakenly believe that being in the cold air can cause you to catch a cold. The primary cause of the "common cold" is actually any one of a variety of airborne viruses spread from person to person. These viruses are most frequently found indoors, in warm, recirculated air. However, exposure to cold air can dry out the mucous membranes of your mouth and nose, which may make it easier for viruses to penetrate when you go indoors. Fitness walking outdoors during cold weather should not cause you to catch a cold as long as you enter a relatively virus-free environment when you go indoors.

When exercising in cold weather it is important to control the amount of heat your body loses. In addition to dressing in layers of clothing, be sure to cover your head and hands. As much as 70 percent of the heat your body loses during cold weather is lost through the head and hands if they are uncovered.

As long as you are healthy and dress warmly, cold weather should not prevent you from enjoying your fitness walking workout.

What precautions should you take before fitness walking in cold weather?

Wet Weather

Many beginning exercisers use wet weather as an excuse to skip an exercise session. Actually, this makes little sense. Human skin is amazingly waterproof, and most exercisers follow their session with a shower anyway. A large number of experienced fitness walkers and joggers enjoy a workout in rain or snow. Remember how much fun it was to play in the rain when you were a child?

If you wish to try to stay dry while walking in the rain, you can wear a waterproof exercise suit. Of course, if you walk vigorously and produce a lot of perspiration, you'll have an especially hard time staying dry. Because the air is already completely saturated with moisture, your perspiration will not evaporate easily on a rainy day. Therefore, you'll still be wet—from perspiration rather than rain. Some water-resistant materials are expensive, but the cost is well worth it if a rain suit will help you stick with your walking program.

Walking in the rain or snow should not be harmful if you take a warm bath or shower, dry thoroughly, and put on warm, dry clothing soon after you finish.

While rain can't hurt you, lightning can. It's one thing to walk in a soft rain shower and another to walk during a violent thunderstorm. If there is lightning outdoors, find a way to exercise indoors for that day.

Rain is no barrier to fitness walking unless it's accompanied by lightning.

Drugs

There is no place in a health improvement program, such as fitness walking, for the use of recreational drugs.

If you are required to take prescription drugs for your health, consult your physician before starting an exercise program. Exercise may alter the effects of the medicine.

Cars

When you are fitness walking outdoors and a car approaches, look directly into the driver's eyes to determine if he or she has seen you. If you suspect that the driver has not seen you it's always best to move out of the way. When a walker and an automobile collide, it obviously does not matter much who was right and who was wrong—the walker will be the loser. Walk on the side of the road facing the oncoming traffic and walk defensively. Make it almost impossible for a car to hit you.

Bicycles

Bicycles are subject to the same traffic laws as cars. Riders should be on the same side of the road and go in the same direction as the motor vehicle traffic. However,

If possible, look directly into the driver's eyes before walking in front of a car.

Give bicyclists the right of way.

if you find yourself on a collision course with a bicycle, it is generally easier for you to move out of the way than for the bicycle rider. Walk defensively. Don't allow a bicycle to hit you.

Dogs

Some fitness walkers encounter problems with loose dogs. No dog should have the right to decide whether you can walk on public property. When you do face such a situation, you have to make your own decision about what to do. Some ideas that have worked for others may also work for you.

If a dog approaches, you probably shouldn't run away. You can't run faster than most dogs, and it may simply encourage the dog to chase you. You also leave

If a dog bothers you, stand your ground, look directly in the dog's eyes, and decide what course of action is safest.

yourself defenseless by turning your back toward the dog. Try not to be intimidated by the dog. Do not panic, but decide what course of action is best for you. You may want to stop, stand your ground, look directly into the dog's eyes, and let the dog know that you are prepared to hurt it if it attacks you. You may choose to slowly back away, still facing the dog. You may slowly walk by, again remembering to face the dog. You may even choose to pick up something to defend yourself, but keep facing the dog.

As a preventive measure you might want to carry something with you when you walk, such as a protective spray or a walking stick. One possible type of walking stick is the shaft of an old golf club with the head removed. It is lightweight, sturdy, and fairly long. It is also relatively sharp on the end, so that it can be used as a protective device as well as a walking stick.

Check the route you want to walk in a car before you walk it the first time. Walk in a group or carry some protection the first time you walk a new course. If there is an area where you want to walk and dogs are running loose, talk to their owners about tying them up or fencing them in. Most communities have laws against dogs running loose. If the owners are uncooperative, call the animal control department or the police. Do not let a dog limit your use of public property.

The same dog should not bother you twice. If it does, it is your fault for not taking steps to remedy the problem the first time.

If you walk at night, wear a reflective vest or tape.

Be especially cautious on potentially dangerous walking surfaces.

Night Walking

It is safer to walk during the daylight hours. However, it's not possible for everyone to walk during the daytime, especially during the winter months when there are fewer daylight hours. If you must walk when it is dark, consider the following safety suggestions:

1. Wear light-colored clothing.
2. Wear a reflective vest or reflective tape on your clothing.
3. Walk in an area with plenty of artificial light.
4. Stay away from dark streets and alleys.
5. Walk with another person or a group.
6. Let someone know your exact route and what time you expect to be back.
7. Wear identification, including the name of the person who should be called in case of an emergency and any medical conditions you have that might affect emergency medical treatment.

Walking Surfaces

Footing is an important consideration for fitness walkers. If you are unsure of a walking surface, slow down and stay alert for dangerous spots.

When walking on pavement, watch for holes and cracks that might cause you to trip. On grass, gravel, and dirt roads, watch for bumps, holes, and sudden differences in firmness. If you are walking indoors on a smooth surface such as wood or tile, be cautious of wet spots, which can be extremely slippery. Finally, if you are walking on a wet or icy surface, shorten your stride, keep your knees slightly bent, and use wider foot placement.

Overtraining

It is possible to get too much exercise. Exercise is a physical stressor that stimulates positive changes to take place in your body. However, if you exercise too much or too often, your body may not be able to recover from the stress. This can lead to muscle soreness, injury, illnesses, and burnout. Adequate rest and proper nutrition are essential to exercise progress and the development of physical fitness.

Following are some symptoms of overtraining:

Sudden, unexpected weight loss	Decreased work capacity
Depression	Poor performance
Insomnia	Loss of enjoyment
Increased resting heart rate	Loss of motivation

If you have several of these symptoms, it's possible that you are overtraining. Try to correct the problem by resting more between exercise sessions, watching your nutritional intake more closely, and reducing the intensity, duration, or frequency of your exercise. If your symptoms were caused by overtraining you should start to feel better within a week or two.

Exercise may do more harm than good if you are overtraining. Each person has an individual rate at which they can best adapt to exercise. This rate changes continually and is influenced by the other stressors in your life. Although general guidelines for exercise exist, you need to listen carefully to your body to find the right amount for you.

Foot Care

The following tips will help you care for your feet.

1. Wear shoes that fit properly (see chapter 3).
2. Wear good quality shoes. Good quality shoes are better for your feet. Since they usually last longer they may not be any more expensive in the long run.

Use weights only when you become an experienced fitness walker.

3. Wear comfortable socks of cotton or cotton blend material that absorb moisture away from your skin.
4. Pay close attention to hot spots on your feet. Hot spots are the first stage of a blister.
5. Keep your feet clean and dry.
6. Keep your toenails properly trimmed.
7. If you have a foot problem, see a medical foot specialist.

Fitness Walking Weights

Some fitness walkers use weights to increase the intensity of their workouts. They generally add a weight vest, ankle weights, wrist weights, or hand weights. While this may not be a problem for the advanced fitness walker, it can be dangerous for the beginner. The additional weight can interfere with your natural walking rhythm, cause unnecessary muscle soreness, and produce an exercise load that is too great for the untrained heart.

Air Pollution

For many people in the United States, air pollution is becoming a serious health problem and exercise hazard. If possible, try to fitness walk in an area with clean air. Air pollution can irritate your lungs and aggravate respiratory conditions such as asthma and bronchitis.

Noise Pollution

Noise pollution may cause additional stress, negating the psychological benefits of fitness walking. Avoid heavy construction sites, congested streets, and large airports. Plan to walk in parks, on running tracks, in quiet neighborhoods, on country roads, or in some other quiet place.

Fitness walking provides many benefits that can improve the quality—and perhaps even the length—of your life. However, it is necessary to take some precautions to make sure your fitness walking program remains safe, enjoyable, and beneficial.

Warm-Up, Cool Down, and Flexibility

5

Warm-Up

Always warm up before fitness walking. A good warm-up can improve your performance and reduce the risk of injury. A proper warm-up for fitness walking requires at least five to ten minutes. It should include gentle stretching and slow walking.

Warm-up stretching should be done gently and carefully. Vigorous stretching of cold muscles can result in injury and muscle soreness. Stretch each joint and each major muscle group through a full range of motion.

The walking portion of your warm-up should begin slowly and gradually increase in speed. Your walking motion will become smoother and easier as your muscles and joints respond to the warm-up.

Warm-up exercises increase muscle temperature and allow your heart rate to increase gradually up to your aerobic exercise heart rate. This safety measure prevents unnecessary cardiac strain.

Group warm-up.

A traditional warm-up method is to perform gentle stretching first, then walking. Another method is to walk slowly for two to five minutes to warm the muscles and joints before stretching. Whether you prefer to warm up by walking or stretching first is a matter of personal preference. Both of these methods are effective. The key is to start slowly and gradually warm up before performing vigorous physical activity.

The warm-up period may also be used to prepare your mind for exercise. It provides a time to focus your attention on your workout and on the development of your body. It is also a time to think about your exercise goals and what you need to accomplish in this exercise session to help you reach those goals. Exercise is more enjoyable and more effective if you have the proper mental attitude for your training session. While you are warming up, think positive thoughts about your workout and rededicate yourself to your exercise goals.

A good warm-up should prepare you physically and mentally for the aerobic portion of your workout.

Cool Down

The cool down is often the most neglected portion of a workout. Many exercisers skip this part of the exercise session. They think that the important part of the workout is finished and the cool down doesn't really matter. Nothing could be farther from the truth.

During the walking portion of your cool down you should gradually reduce your walking speed. This should result in a gradual reduction in oxygen demand, which will allow your heart to slowly return toward its resting rate.

The rhythmic contraction of your skeletal muscles helps your heart maintain adequate circulation during exercise. As you walk and your skeletal muscles rhythmically contract, your veins are alternately squeezed and released. This milking action forces the blood in your veins to move toward your heart. Your blood doesn't flow back in the other direction because of blood pressure, and because of one-way valves in the veins that allow blood to flow only toward your heart.

Rhythmic skeletal muscle contractions provide as much as 30 percent of the force necessary to circulate your blood during vigorous physical activity. If you are exercising vigorously and stop suddenly, these important rhythmic muscle contractions also stop. Blood may then accumulate in your veins, especially in your legs. This sudden increase in workload for your heart may occur at a time when there is less blood returning to it. Therefore, you should continue walking for a few minutes after the aerobic portion of your workout while gradually reducing your walking speed.

Your cool down should generally last at least five to ten minutes. Like the warm-up, it should include slow walking and stretching. The length of your cool down depends upon how vigorously you have been exercising and the physical condition you are in. The more vigorous the exercise, the longer it takes to cool down, and the less fit you are, the longer it takes to cool down.

Flexibility

Flexibility is the amount of movement, or range of motion, that exists at each joint. Limited range of joint motion can limit performance in some activities and increase the risk of soft tissue injury. Increased flexibility is a healthy goal for most people.

Stretching to improve flexibility is best done after the aerobic portion of your workout when the soft tissues (muscles, tendons, and ligaments) are warm and the joints are well lubricated.

Static stretching is recommended for the following reasons:

It is an effective method of increasing flexibility.
It involves less risk of injury to the soft tissues that are being stretched.
It helps prevent muscle soreness.
It helps relieve muscle soreness.
It is easy to learn.
It can be done without a partner.

General Tips for Stretching to Increase Flexibility

1. Use static stretch. To perform a static stretch, move a joint to the limit of its normal range of motion. Then, gently apply pressure to move the joint slightly beyond the point where it normally stops. Hold this position. Do not bounce.
2. Stretch to the point of moderate discomfort. You should be able to feel which muscle, or group of muscles, is being stretched, but it should not be painful. Hold this position.
3. Hold each static stretch for ten to thirty seconds. Repeat each stretch one to three times.
4. Do not injure the soft tissues. You should not experience extreme discomfort or pain while stretching. If you experience extreme pain, you are stretching too far.
5. Breathe slowly, rhythmically, and comfortably while stretching. Do not hold your breath. If you cannot breathe normally while stretching, you are probably stretching too far.
6. Stretch any time you feel tightness. Stretching does not have to be restricted to your workout.
7. Keep warm-up stretches with cold muscles and joints light and easy.
8. Be sure your muscles are completely warmed up before performing stretching exercises to increase flexibility. Walk for a few minutes after you have completed the aerobic portion of your workout to allow your heart rate to return toward its resting level. Then stretch your muscles. (They will stay warm for a long time after exercise.)
9. Make stretching a relaxing daily habit. Some people like to stretch when they get up in the morning; some like to stretch before going to bed at night. Some people stretch before and after daily exercise. Stretching improves performance and reduces the risk of injury.

Anterior shoulder stretch.   Posterior shoulder stretch.

Why is it important to be sure your muscles are warmed up before stretching to improve flexibility? How do stretches in a warm-up differ from stretches performed to increase flexibility?

Ten Stretches for Fitness Walking

1. **Anterior Shoulder Stretch** Start in a standing position. With your hands behind your back, join the fingers of both hands together. Straighten both arms and raise your hands as high as possible behind your back. Hold this position.
2. **Posterior Shoulder Stretch** Start in a standing position. Place your right arm over your head with your elbow bent. Grasp your right elbow with your left hand and gently pull your right elbow and upper arm behind your head. Hold this position. Repeat this exercise with the left arm.
3. **Side Stretch** Stand with your feet shoulder width apart. Place both arms straight above your head and lean to the left. Stretch all of the muscles along the right side of your body. Hold this position. Repeat this exercise, leaning to the right.
4. **Adductor Stretch** Start in a standing position with your feet apart two to three times your shoulder width. Bend your right knee slightly and stretch

Side stretch.   Adductor stretch.

the muscles along the inside of your left thigh. Hold this position. Repeat this exercise with your left knee slightly bent, stretching the muscles along the inside of your right thigh.

5. **Lunge Stretch** From a standing position take a large step forward with your left leg. Bend the knee of your forward leg, keeping your feet pointed straight ahead. With your upper body erect and your arms out to the sides for balance, slowly press down and forward with your hips, stretching the muscles that cross the front of the hip joint. Draw your arms backward, stretching the shoulder muscles at the same time. Hold this position. Repeat this exercise with the right leg forward.

6. **Hamstring Stretch** Start by lying on your back with your knees bent and both feet flat on the floor. Raise your right leg with your knee bent. Grasp the ball of the right foot with your right hand. Place your left hand behind your right knee. Pull your right thigh toward your chest while trying to straighten your leg at the knee. Hold this position. Repeat this exercise, using the opposite leg.

7. **Low Back Stretch** Start by lying on your back with both legs straight. Pull one thigh toward your chest with your knee bent and both hands behind your thigh. Hold this position. Repeat this exercise, using the opposite leg.

8. **Knees-to-Chest Stretch** Start by lying on your back with your knees bent and both feet flat on the floor. Bring both knees toward your chest. Grasp the backs of both thighs and pull your knees toward your chest, curling your upper body forward. Hold this position.

Lunge stretch.

Low back stretch.

Knees-to-chest stretch.

Hamstring stretch.

Ankle stretch.

Calf stretch.

9. **Calf Stretch** Stand facing a wall, approximately three feet away from it, with your feet about twelve inches apart. Lean forward from the ankles and place your hands on the wall, keeping your body and your legs straight. Lean forward as far as possible while keeping your feet flat on the floor. Hold this position.

10. **Ankle Circle Stretch** Stand on your left foot. Rotate your right foot at the ankle, going clockwise three times, then counterclockwise three times. Repeat this exercise with the left foot.

Warm-up, cool down, and flexibility stretches are important components of your fitness walking program. All three contribute to greater safety and improved performance.

___

Activity 5a

The purpose of this activity is for you to learn flexibility exercises that may be used as part of your fitness walking program.

Perform each of the ten fitness walking stretches listed in this chapter. Follow the general tips for stretching.

Fitness Walking Test

6

What is your present cardiovascular fitness level? Have you measured it? Would you like to measure it? There is now a walking test that can be used to measure your cardiovascular fitness level. The Rockport Fitness Walking Test is a scientifically validated field test of cardiovascular fitness using walking.

Knowing your current fitness level can help you find a realistic place to start your fitness walking program. By starting at the appropriate exercise level, you can make your walking program safer, more productive, and more enjoyable.

If you have not exercised in a long time be very cautious about taking any fitness test. Do not push yourself too hard during the test. It is much safer to complete the test comfortably and be classified in a lower fitness category than to push yourself too hard and risk injury. Some experts recommend beginning with a low intensity starter program for at least two or three weeks before taking any fitness test.

Many people start exercise programs with unrealistic expectations. They start out highly motivated and full of enthusiasm, but with little knowledge of their present fitness level or the amount of exercise they need. Consequently, they frequently start out doing too much. This often leads to muscle soreness, fatigue, frustration, injury, or burnout. Most of these people then lose their motivation and quit exercising.

It is unrealistic to think you can make up for years of bad habits in a few days. The benefits of regular exercise come from a lifetime habit of moderate exercise. It is better to start at a comfortable level of fitness walking and enjoy it for the rest of your life than to exercise at a high level for a few days and quit.

To prevent this from occurring, test yourself. Assessing your fitness level enables you to start on the fitness walking program that best fits your needs and present physical condition. You will be able to enjoy your walking program while you progress gradually and safely.

Medical Clearance

Before taking the fitness walking test, make sure it is medically safe for you to participate. Read the medical clearance section in chapter 4 and complete Activity 4a before taking the Rockport Fitness Walking Test.

Why the Rockport Fitness Walking Test?

Researchers at the University of Massachusetts Medical School found that cardiovascular fitness could be estimated fairly accurately using four factors: age, sex, time to walk one-mile, and heart rate at the completion of a one-mile walk.

The researchers developed charts for estimating cardiovascular fitness levels using these four factors and fitness norms from the American Heart Association. This field test of cardiovascular fitness is called the Rockport Fitness Walking Test.

How to Take the Rockport Fitness Walking Test

To take the Rockport Fitness Walking Test, you need to learn to count your heart rate. Gently place the fingertips of your index finger and middle finger on the radial artery. You will find this artery on the palm side of your forearm just above your wrist. You can also count your pulse by placing the same two fingertips on the carotid artery. You will find this artery by placing your fingertips along the side of your trachea near the top.

Use either the carotid artery or radial artery to count your pulse.

The purpose of this activity is to learn how to count your pulse at the radial artery and the carotid artery.

You need to know how to count your pulse before taking the Rockport Fitness Walking Test. Read or review the section in this chapter that explains how to count your pulse to determine your heart rate.

Find your pulse within five seconds and count it for fifteen seconds. Practice three times using the radial artery and three times using the carotid artery.

To convert your pulse count to a heart rate in beats per minute, multiply each fifteen-second count times four.

To take the walking test, you need a watch that can measure your time in minutes and seconds. Find a flat, measured mile to walk. The quarter-mile track at a local school is an excellent place. If no track is available, measure a one-mile course where you can walk continuously and uninterrupted. Avoid traffic and stoplights. It is a good idea to measure a half-mile so you can walk out and back. That way you will know when you are halfway through the test, and you will end up where you started.

Walk the mile as fast as you can—running is not allowed. However, do not walk so fast that you endanger your health. Slow down if the pace is too severe.

To determine your current fitness level, two measurements are necessary. One is the time it takes you to walk one mile in minutes and seconds. The other is your heart rate immediately after finishing the mile.

When you cross the finish line, record your time in minutes and seconds. Within five seconds after you finish, locate your pulse and count the number of pulse beats in fifteen seconds. Multiply this number times four to determine your exercise heart rate in beats per minute. The reason for locating your pulse immediately and taking a short, fifteen-second pulse count is to find your exercise heart rate. A great deal of recovery can occur within the first minute after you stop exercising. Therefore, if you wait too long to locate your pulse, or take a longer count, your test results will not be valid.

How to Find Your Fitness Category

Once your results are recorded, you can determine your current fitness level by looking at the appropriate fitness level chart for your age and sex. The twenty-to-twenty-nine-year-old relative fitness charts can be used for college students under the age of twenty.

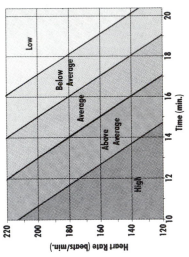

20-29

20-29 Year Old Males
Relative Fitness Level

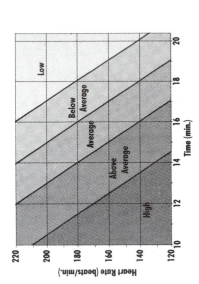

20-29 Year Old Females
Relative Fitness Level

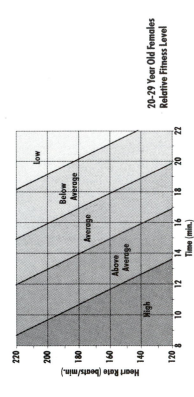

30-39

30-39 Year Old Males
Relative Fitness Level

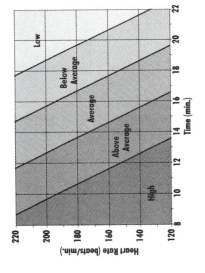

30-39 Year Old Females
Relative Fitness Level

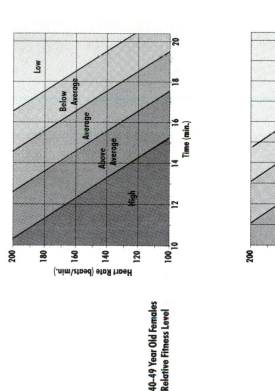

**40-49 Year Old Males
Relative Fitness Level**

**40-49 Year Old Females
Relative Fitness Level**

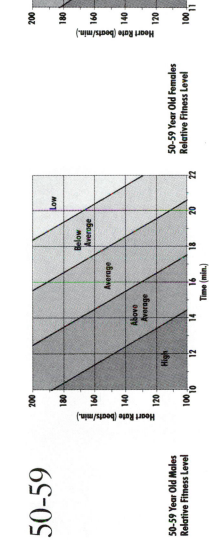

**50-59 Year Old Males
Relative Fitness Level**

**50-59 Year Old Females
Relative Fitness Level**

Relative fitness level charts.

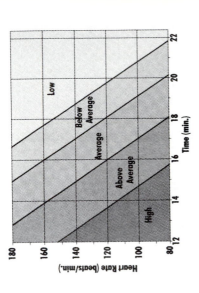

**60 + Year Old Females
Relative Fitness Level**

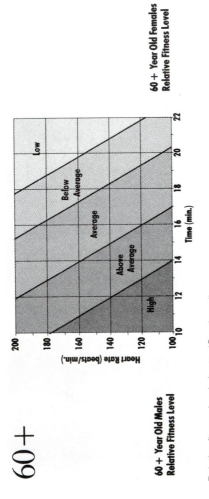

60+

**60 + Year Old Males
Relative Fitness Level**

Relative fitness level charts. (Continued)

Activity 6b

The purpose of this activity is to determine your current fitness level using the Rockport Fitness Walking Test. Make sure you have read the medical and safety guidelines before taking the test.

Follow the directions for the Rockport Fitness Walking Test. When you finish, record your results. Once your results are recorded, follow the directions in this chapter to find your fitness category.

Age _____ Sex _____
One-Mile Walk Time (in minutes and seconds) _____
Exercise Heart Rate: 15 Seconds _____ × 4 = _____ BPM
Fitness Category _____

On the horizontal line at the bottom of the chart locate the time it took you to complete the one-mile walk. Place a mark on the line at that point. On the vertical line at the left side of the chart locate your exercise heart rate in beats per minute. Draw one line straight up from your time and another line straight across from your heart rate. The point at which the two lines intersect indicates your cardiovascular fitness level.

Retesting

How often should you retest yourself on the Rockport Fitness Walking Test? Ideally, it is best to wait until you finish each twenty-week fitness walking program. The most important benefits come from a consistent and lifelong fitness walking program. When you retest yourself too frequently, you tend to focus your attention on short-term changes. Although short-term changes are interesting, long-term benefits are more important.

When you retest after completing a twenty-week fitness walking program, you may find that you have moved up a fitness level. If that is the case, plan your next fitness walking program based on your new fitness level.

When you reach a satisfactory cardiovascular fitness level, change to a maintenance walking program. Taking the walking test two or three times a year should be sufficient once you are on a maintenance program. However, there are some regular walkers who prefer to take the test once a month. This helps them monitor their fitness level on a regular basis and provides motivation for them to keep up with their exercise program.

Fitness Walking Programs

7

Exercise is like medicine. Both can be good for you if you get the right kind and the right amount. Fitness walking is the right kind of exercise for most people. This chapter will help you select the right amount.

Rockport Walking Programs

If you have completed the Rockport Fitness Walking Test you are ready to select your fitness walking program. The Rockport Walking Programs correspond to your current cardiovascular fitness level as measured by the Rockport Fitness Walking Test.

Find the appropriate exercise program chart for your age and sex. The 20 to 29 year-old exercise program charts can be used for college students under the age of twenty.

On the horizontal line at the bottom of the chart, locate the time it took you to complete the one-mile walk. Place a mark on the line at that point. On the vertical line at the left side of the chart, locate your exercise heart rate at the end of the one-mile walk. Draw one line straight up from your time and another line straight across from your heart rate. The point at which the two lines intersect indicates which exercise program is appropriate for you based upon your current fitness level.

Rockport Exercise Programs

These programs were developed by the cardiologists and exercise scientists from the Exercise Physiology Lab and Department of Exercise Science at the University of Massachusetts Medical School using extensive field data. They are designed to help maintain or improve your level of fitness, depending on your current level. For best results, follow the programs closely.

At the end of each twenty-week period, retake the Rockport Fitness Walking Test to determine your new fitness level and exercise program.

On each program you'll see columns labelled "Pace" and"Heart Rate." The pace listed is only an approximation. Walking speed should be the pace that keeps your heart rate at the appropriate percentage listed. To determine your maximum heart rate, subtract your age from 220.

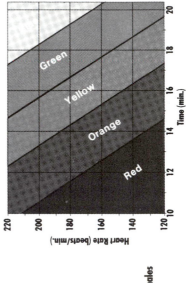

20-29 Year Old Females
Exercise Program

30-39 Year Old Females
Exercise Program

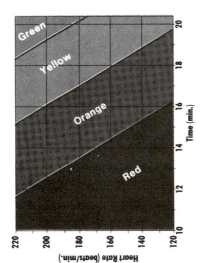

20-29 Year Old Males
Exercise Program

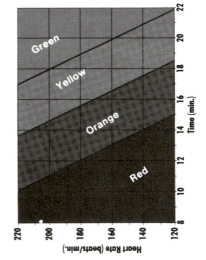

30-39 Year Old Males
Exercise Program

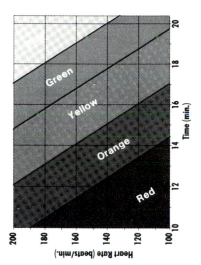

**40-49 Year Old Females
Exercise Program**

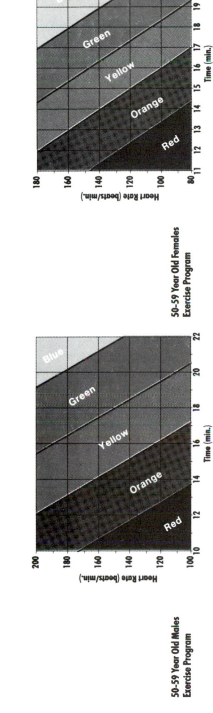

**50-59 Year Old Females
Exercise Program**

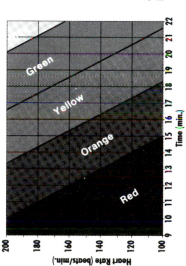

**40-49 Year Old Males
Exercise Program**

**50-59 Year Old Males
Exercise Program**

Exercise Program Charts.

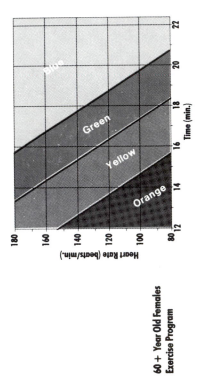

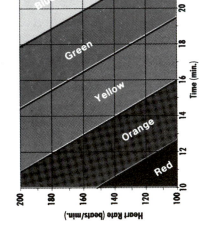

60 + Year Old Males Exercise Program

60 + Year Old Females Exercise Program

Table 7.1 Low-Level Fitness Program. (Blue)

Week	Warm-up	Mileage	Pace (mph)	Heart Rate (% of max.)	Cool-down	Frequency (times per week)
1	5–7 mins. before-walk stretches	1.0	3.0	60	5–7 mins. after-walk stretches	5
2	5–7 mins.	1.0	3.0	60	5–7 mins.	5
3	5–7 mins.	1.25	3.0	60	5–7 mins.	5
4	5–7 mins.	1.25	3.0	60	5–7 mins.	5
5	5–7 mins.	1.5	3.0	60	5–7 mins.	5
6	5–7 mins.	1.5	3.5	60–70	5–7 mins.	5
7	5–7 mins.	1.75	3.5	60–70	5–7 mins.	5
8	5–7 mins.	1.75	3.5	60–70	5–7 mins.	5
9	5–7 mins.	2.0	3.5	60–70	5–7 mins.	5
10	5–7 mins.	2.0	3.75	60–70	5–7 mins.	5
11	5–7 mins.	2.0	3.75	70	5–7mins.	5
12	5–7 mins.	2.25	3.75	70	5–7mins.	5
13	5–7 mins.	2.25	3.75	70	5–7 mins.	5
14	5–7 mins.	2.5	3.75	70	5–7 mins.	5
15	5–7 mins.	2.5	4.0	70	5–7 mins.	5
16	5–7 mins.	2.5	4.0	70	5–7 mins.	5
17	5–7 mins.	2.75	4.0	70–80	5–7 mins.	5
18	5–7 mins.	2.75	4.0	70–80	5–7 mins.	5
19	5–7 mins.	3.0	4.0	70–80	5–7 mins.	5
20	5–7 mins.	3.0	4.0	70–80	5–7 mins.	5

At the end of the twenty-week fitness walking protocol, retest yourself to establish your new program.

Table 7.2   Below-Average Level Fitness Program. (Green)

Week	Warm-up	Mileage	Pace (mph)	Heart Rate (% of max.)	Cool-down	Frequency (times per week)
1	5–7 mins. before-walk stretches	1.5	3.0	60–70	5–7 mins. after-walk stretches	5
2	5–7 mins.	1.5	3.0	60–70	5–7 mins.	5
3	5–7 mins.	1.75	3.0	60–70	5–7 mins.	5
4	5–7 mins.	1.75	3.0	60–70	5–7 mins.	5
5	5–7 mins.	2.0	3.0	60–70	5–7 mins.	5
6	5–7 mins.	2.0	3.0	60–70	5–7 mins.	5
7	5–7 mins.	2.0	3.5	70	5–7 mins.	5
8	5–7 mins.	2.25	3.5	70	5–7 mins.	5
9	5–7 mins.	2.25	3.5	70	5–7 mins.	5
10	5–7 mins.	2.5	3.5	70	5–7 mins.	5
11	5–7 mins.	2.5	3.5	70	5–7 mins.	5
12	5–7 mins.	2.5	3.5	70	5–7 mins.	5
13	5–7 mins.	2.75	3.5	70	5–7 mins.	5
14	5–7 mins.	2.75	4.0	70–80	5–7 mins.	5
15	5–7 mins.	3.0	4.0	70–80	5–7 mins.	5
16	5–7 mins.	3.0	4.0	70–80	5–7 mins.	5
17	5–7 mins.	3.25	4.0	70–80	5–7 mins.	5
18	5–7 mins.	3.25	4.0	70–80	5–7 mins.	5
19	5–7 mins.	3.5	4.0	70–80	5–7 mins.	5
20	5–7 mins.	3.5	4.0	70–80	5–7 mins.	5

At the end of the twenty-week fitness walking protocol, retest yourself to establish your new program.

Table 7.3 Average-Level Fitness Program. (Yellow)

Week	Warm-up	Mileage	Pace (mph)	Heart Rate (% of max.)	Cool-down	Frequency (times per week)
1	5–7 mins. before-walk stretches	2.0	3.0	70	5–7 mins. after-walk stretches	5
2	5–7 mins.	2.25	3.0	70	5–7 mins.	5
3	5–7 mins.	2.5	3.0	70	5–7 mins.	5
4	5–7 mins.	2.5	3.0	70	5–7 mins.	5
5	5–7 mins.	2.75	3.0	70	5–7 mins.	5
6	5–7 mins.	2.75	3.5	70	5–7 mins.	5
7	5–7 mins.	2.75	3.5	70	5–7 mins.	5
8	5–7 mins.	2.75	3.5	70	5–7 mins.	5
9	5–7 mins.	3.0	3.5	70	5–7 mins.	5
10	5–7 mins.	3.0	3.5	70	5–7 mins.	5
11	5–7 mins.	3.0	4.0	70–80	5–7 mins.	5
12	5–7 mins.	3.0	4.0	70–80	5–7 mins.	5
13	5–7 mins.	3.25	4.0	70–80	5–7 mins.	5
14	5–7 mins.	3.25	4.0	70–80	5–7 mins.	5
15	5–7 mins.	3.5	4.0	70–80	5–7 mins.	5
16	5–7 mins.	3.5	4.5	70–80	5–7 mins.	5
17	5–7 mins.	3.5	4.5	70–80	5–7 mins.	5
18	5–7 mins.	4.0	4.5	70–80	5–7 mins.	5
19	5–7 mins.	4.0	4.5	70–80	5–7 mins.	5
20	5–7 mins.	4.0	4.5	70–80	5–7 mins.	5

At the end of the twenty-week fitness walking protocol you may either retest yourself and move to a new fitness walking category or begin the Average-Level Fitness Maintenance Program for a lifetime of fitness walking.

Table 7.4   Above-Average Level Fitness Program. (Orange)

Week	Warm-up	Mileage	Pace (mph)	Incline or Weight	Heart Rate (% of max.)	Cool-down	Frequency (times per week)
1	5–7 mins. before-walk stretches	2.5	3.5		70	5–7 mins. after-walk stretches	5
2	5–7 mins.	2.75	3.5		70	5–7 mins.	5
3	5–7 mins.	3.0	3.5		70	5–7 mins.	5
4	5–7 mins.	3.0	3.5		70	5–7 mins.	5
5	5–7 mins.	3.25	3.5		70	5–7 mins.	5
6	5–7 mins.	3.25	4.0		70–80	5–7 mins.	5
7	5–7 mins.	3.5	4.0		70–80	5–7 mins.	5
8	5–7 mins.	3.75	4.0		70–80	5–7 mins.	5
9	5–7 mins.	4.0	4.0		70–80	5–7 mins.	5
10	5–7 mins.	4.0	4.0		70–80	5–7 mins.	5
11	5–7 mins.	4.0	4.5		70–80	5–7 mins.	5
12	5–7 mins.	4.0	4.5		70–80	5–7 mins.	5
13	5–7 mins.	4.0	4.5		70–80	5–7 mins.	5
14	5–7 mins.	4.0	4.5		70–80	5–7 mins.	5
15	5–7 mins.	4.0	4.5	+	70–80	5–7 mins.	3
16	5–7 mins.	4.0	4.5	+	70–80	5–7 mins.	3
17	5–7 mins.	4.0	4.5	+	70–80	5–7 mins.	3
18	5–7 mins.	4.0	4.5	+	70–80	5–7 mins.	3
19	5–7 mins.	4.0	4.5	+	70–80	5–7 mins.	3
20	5–7 mins.	4.0	4.5	+	70–80	5–7 mins.	3

At the end of the twenty-week fitness walking protocol begin the Above-Average/High-Level Fitness Maintenance Program for a lifetime of fitness walking.

Table 7.5   High-Level Fitness Program. (Red)

Week	Warm-up	Mileage	Pace (mph)	Incline or Weight	Heart Rate (% of max.)	Cool-down	Frequency (times per week)
1	5–7 mins. before-walk stretches	3.0	4.0		70	5–7 mins. after-walk stretches	5
2	5–7 mins.	3.25	4.0	No	70	5–7 mins.	5
3	5–7 mins.	3.5	4.0	No	70	5–7 mins.	5
4	5–7 mins.	3.5	4.5	No	70–80	5–7 mins.	5
5	5–7 mins.	3.75	4.5	No	70–80	5–7 mins.	5
6	5–7 mins.	4.0	4.5	No	70–80	5–7 mins.	5
7	5–7 mins.	4.0	4.5	+	70–80	5–7 mins.	3
8	5–7 mins.	4.0	4.5	+	70–80	5–7 mins.	3
9	5–7 mins.	4.0	4.5	+	70–80	5–7 mins.	3
10	5–7 mins.	4.0	4.5	+	70–80	5–7 mins.	3
11	5–7 mins.	4.0	4.5	+	70–80	5–7 mins.	3
12	5–7 mins.	4.0	4.5	+	70–80	5–7 mins.	3
13	5–7 mins.	4.0	4.5	+	70–80	5–7 mins.	3
14	5–7 mins.	4.0	4.5	+	70–80	5–7 mins.	3
15	5–7 mins.	4.0	4.5	+	70–80	5–7 mins.	3
16	5–7 mins.	4.0	4.5	+	70–80	5–7 mins.	3
17	5–7 mins.	4.0	4.5	+	70–80	5–7 mins.	3
18	5–7 mins.	4.0	4.5	+	70–80	5–7 mins.	3
19	5–7 mins.	4.0	4.5	+	70–80	5–7 mins.	3
20	5–7 mins.	4.0	4.5	+	70–80	5–7 mins.	3

At the end of the twenty-week fitness walking protocol begin the Above Average/High Level Fitness Maintenance Program for a lifetime of fitness walking.

Yellow Maintenance Program

Warm-up: 5–7 minutes before walk stretches

Aerobic work out: mileage: 4.0 pace: 4.5 mph

Heart rate: 70–80% of maximum

Cooldown: 5–7 minutes after walk stretches

Frequency: 3–5 times per week

Weekly mileage: 12–20 miles

Warm-up: 5–7 minutes before walk stretches

Aerobic work out: mileage: 4.0 pace: 4.5 mph
     weight/incline: add weights to upper body or add hill walking as needed to keep heart rate in target zone (70–80% of predicted maximum).

Heart rate: 70–80% of maximum

Cooldown: 5–7 minutes after walk stretches

Frequency: 3–5 times per week

Weekly mileage: 12–20 miles

Guidelines for Planning Personal Fitness Walking Programs

The preplanned Rockport Fitness Walking Programs are excellent. However, some fitness walkers may want to plan their own fitness walking programs. The following guidelines will help you plan your own program.

The Right Kind of Exercise

Why is fitness walking the right kind of exercise? Aerobic exercise is the best type to develop your cardiovascular system, reduce your risk of cardiovascular disease, and reduce the amount of stored body fat you have accumulated. Aerobic exercises are exercises that require you to use large amounts of oxygen for an extended period of time. Exercises that use large muscle groups in a rhythmic and continuous manner work best. Fitness walking is an excellent aerobic exercise.

The Right Amount of Exercise

The right amount of exercise is determined by its intensity, duration, and frequency.

Intensity

Intensity refers to how hard you need to exercise to benefit from each training session. How fast do you need to walk? Your exercise heart rate provides a good indication of how hard you are exercising. A good guideline for fitness walking is to reach an exercise heart rate between 60 and 90 percent of your maximum heart rate. You can estimate your maximum heart rate by subtracting your age from 220.

 Beginning fitness walkers should start out at a low intensity, about 60 to 70 percent of their maximum heart rate. Only advanced fitness walkers should attempt to exercise at high intensity (80 to 90 percent of their maximum heart rate).

Activity 7a

The purpose of this activity is to determine your exercise heart rate range. This will help you monitor your exercise intensity.

Calculate your exercise heart rate range following the instructions in the section on intensity in this chapter.

Duration

How long do you need to walk? You should walk for fifteen to sixty minutes at your prescribed exercise heart rate. If you are just starting a fitness walking program, keep the intensity low and the duration short. Gradually increase the duration, then the intensity.

Frequency

How often should you walk? Fitness walking must be performed regularly to be effective. The recommended frequency for fitness walking is three to five days per week. Some people on a weight loss program may benefit from walking six or seven days per week.

Recovery

How much exercise is too much? As a general guideline, if you experience extreme muscle soreness the next day and cannot repeat your fitness walking workout, you have done too much and need to reduce the amount you exercise the next time.

Exercise is only the stimulus for positive biological changes to occur in your body. These changes actually occur during the recovery time between exercise sessions. Make sure the exercise stimulus is not too severe and that you get adequate rest and nutrition between walking workouts.

Some people believe the old athletic myth "no pain, no gain." They actually believe that you must work until you are in pain for exercise to be beneficial. Of course, this is one of the reasons many people do not exercise regularly. Most people do not look forward to painful experiences, but instead try to avoid them.

One problem common among middle-aged people is that they desire to get back into the physical condition they were in when they were young. This is generally not a realistic expectation.

Many people who have been inactive for a long time want to get in shape fast. Biological adaptation is a relatively slow process. You cannot expect to reverse the effects of years of sedentary living in a few days or weeks. Don't fall into the trap of thinking that if a little bit of exercise is good, more must be better. This is only true to a point. Beyond that point, additional exercise can be harmful. Follow the exercise guidelines. Progress slowly and safely. If you try to progress too quickly you are likely to become injured and to lose your motivation to exercise. If you quit, you will not achieve the benefits that come from regular exercise.

If you are exercising for health, you do not need to keep improving forever. When you reach the fitness level you want, change to a walking program that will keep you at that level.

The boxed guidelines will help you select a safe and enjoyable walking program that you can stay with and benefit from for the rest of your life.

Guidelines for Fitness Walking to Develop Cardiovascular Fitness

The Right Kind of Exercise—Fitness Walking
The Right Amount of Exercise
    Intensity—60 to 90 percent of maximum heart rate
    Duration—15 to 60 minutes
    Frequency—3 to 7 days per week

Because it is simpler, some people prefer this program to the Rockport program. If you follow these guidelines, all you need to keep track of is the total minutes you walked at your exercise heart rate. This method also gives you greater freedom to walk new courses, since you do not need to know the exact distance you are walking.

American Heart Association Walking Program

The American Heart Association offers a program that is excellent for beginners who are not regular exercisers. Each workout should consist of a warmup, a walk within the target heart rate zone, and a cool down. You are to keep your exercise heart rate between 60 and 75 percent of your maximum and walk at least three times each week.

Week	Target Zone Exercising	Total Time in Minutes (warm up + target zone exercising + cool down)
1	Walk briskly 5 min.	15 min.
2	Walk briskly 7 min.	17 min.
3	Walk briskly 9 min.	19 min.
4	Walk briskly 11 min.	21 min.
5	Walk briskly 13 min.	23 min.
6	Walk briskly 15 min.	25 min.
7	Walk briskly 18 min.	28 min.
8	Walk briskly 20 min.	30 min.
9	Walk briskly 23 min.	33 min.
10	Walk briskly 26 min.	36 min.
11	Walk briskly 28 min.	38 min.
12	Walk briskly 30 min.	40 min.
13 on:	Check your pulse periodicially to see if you are exercising within your target zone. As you get more in shape, try exercising within the upper range of your target heart zone. Remember that your goal is to continue getting the benefits you seek while enjoying your activity.	

Reproduced with permission. WALKING FOR A HEALTHY HEART American Heart Association

Total Health-Related Physical Fitness

Total health-related physical fitness includes cardiovascular endurance, muscular endurance, strength, flexibility, and body composition.

Cardiovascular Endurance

Cardiovascular endurance refers to your ability to continue vigorous total body activity for a relatively long period of time. To develop cardiovascular endurance, perform exercises that use large muscle groups in a rhythmic and continuous manner. Maintain an exercise heart rate that is 60 to 90 percent of your maximum heart rate for fifteen to sixty minutes, and repeat this workout three to seven times each week.

Muscle Endurance

Muscle endurance refers to the ability of individual muscles or muscle groups to exert force for many repetitions, or to hold a position for an extended period of time. To develop muscle endurance, perform exercises that require movement through a full range of motion against resistance. Use a resistance that is 50 to 70 percent of your maximum voluntary contraction (one repetition maximum) and execute twenty to thirty repetitions. Perform one to three sets of each exercise and repeat your muscle endurance exercises three to five days per week.

Strength

Strength refers to the amount of force a muscle can exert. To develop strength, perform exercises that involve movement through a full range of motion against resistance. Use a resistance that is 70 to 100 percent of the heaviest weight you can lift, or of your maximum voluntary contraction (one repetition maximum) and execute one to ten repetitions. Perform one to three sets of each exercise and repeat your strength training program three days per week.

Flexibility

Flexibility refers to the range of motion available at a joint. To develop flexibility, use slow, static stretch exercises. Stretch to the point of moderate discomfort, hold each stretch for ten to thirty seconds, and perform each stretch one to three times. Repeat your stretching program three to seven days per week.

Body Composition

Body composition refers to the tissues your body is composed of. The particular concern is how much of your body is stored body fat. The best exercises to reduce stored body fat are those that use large muscle groups in a rhythmic and continuous manner. Exercise at a heart rate that is 60 to 90 percent of your heart rate range for thirty to sixty minutes. Repeat this workout five to seven days per week.

Total Health-Related Physical Fitness Program

Fitness walking programs, including the stretching exercises performed during the warm-up and cool down, develop cardiovascular endurance, muscular endurance, flexibility, and body composition. Adding a few strength exercises after the walking portion, and before the stretching portion, of your cool down, would result in a total health-related physical fitness program.

A total health-related physical fitness walking program should include the following:

—Warm-up stretching (gentle stretch)
—Warm-up walking
—Fitness walking at exercise heart rate
—Cool down walking
—Strength and muscle endurance exercises
—Cool down stretching (flexibility stretching)

Fitness Walking Techniques

This chapter explains some specific walking techniques that will increase your speed, stride length, and efficiency. You will also improve your balance, coordination, body control, posture, and agility as you learn these techniques.

Once you have learned the proper form, your pace will become faster. Your heart and lungs will have to work harder to supply necessary oxygen to the working muscles. This will improve your cardiovascular conditioning.

Even after you have learned these walking techniques and have become a regular fitness walker, you will probably need to return to this chapter to review the techniques and refine your walking skill. The most experienced fitness walkers continue to review and improve their walking techniques.

Learn one walking technique at a time. Focus on one technique during each workout. Practice each technique until it becomes automatic.

Technique 1: Posture and Alignment

For the smoothest walking motion, maintain correct posture and body alignment. Apply the guidelines listed in Activity 8a while you walk.

Activity 8a

The purpose of this activity is to learn correct body alignment for fitness walking.

Assume a standing position with correct body alignment for fitness walking. Have a partner evaluate each guideline and place a check in either the yes or no column.

Guidelines	Yes	No
Head and neck erect	___	___
Eyes straight ahead	___	___
Shoulders pulled back and relaxed	___	___
Back straight	___	___
Chest lifted up	___	___
Abdomen pulled in	___	___
Buttocks tucked in	___	___
Elbows down at side	___	___
Elbows bent at 90-degree angle	___	___
Palms facing inward	___	___
Hands in relaxed fist position	___	___

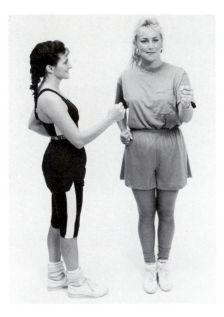

Technique 1: Posture and alignment.

Technique 2: Heel contact.

Technique 2: Heel Contact

From the correct posture position, swing one leg forward. Land on the outer edge of your heel with the bottom of your foot at about a 40-degree angle to the ground. Make sure your heel contacts the ground first. Do not land flat-footed or on the ball of your foot.

Activity 8b

The purpose of this activity is to practice landing on your heel first, as opposed to landing flat-footed or on the ball of your foot.

Read the section on technique number two; heel contact. Walk ten steps. Ask a partner to check to see if you are contacting the ground with your heel first. Your foot should also be at approximately a 40-degree angle to the ground when your heel makes contact.

Technique 3: Heel-to-Toe Roll

Once your heel makes contact with the ground, begin to roll your foot forward, keeping your weight toward the outer edge of your foot until your toes touch the ground. The outer edge of your foot acts as a natural rocker bottom for continuous forward motion. As you roll your foot forward with your weight toward the outer edge, keep your knees pointing straight ahead.

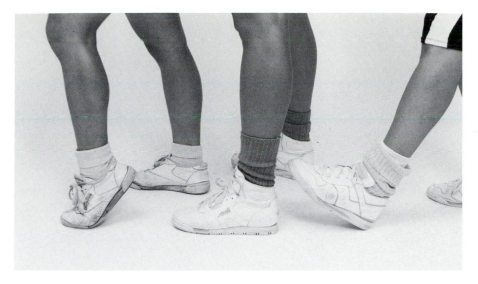

Technique 3: Heel-to-toe roll.

Activity 8c

The purpose of this activity is to experience the heel-to-toe roll.

Read technique number three: heel-to-toe-roll. Walk ten steps. Ask a partner to watch your heel-to-toe roll. After your heel makes contact with the ground, roll your foot forward. Keep the weight toward the outer edge of your foot. Continue to roll forward until you push off with your toes.

Technique 4: Push Off

Following the heel-to-toe roll, continue your forward motion with a push off from your toes. Resist the temptation to pick your foot up early, as you might in casual walking. Keep your foot in contact with the ground as long as possible. You can lengthen your stride on each step by pushing off with your toes.

To reduce excesive side-to-side swaying, and avoid putting undue stress on your joints, keep your support foot pointing straight ahead. If your body rises and falls with each step, you may be pushing off from the front part of your foot instead of your toes. If this happens, reduce your speed and focus on the push off.

Walk ten steps with a good push-off from the toes; then walk ten steps without using the toes at all. What difference does the absence of the toe push-off make in your stride?

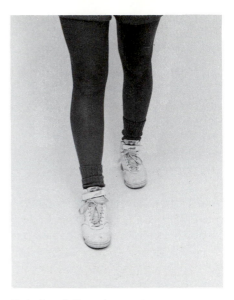

Technique 4: Push off.

Technique 5: Foot placement.

To receive the greatest benefits from fitness walking, it is necessary to walk at a brisk pace. A longer stride will help you walk faster since you will be able to cover more ground in fewer steps.

You may need to perform stretching exercises to improve your ankle, foot, and toe flexibility for a greater range of motion on the push off.

Activity 8d

The purpose of this activity is to practice the push off.

Read technique number four: push off. Raise yourself on the toes of both feet at the same time. Repeat this five times. Next, practice the push off by walking a short distance with an exaggerated push off. Push all the way up on your toes before breaking contact with the ground. Ask a partner to watch to see if you are pushing off with your toes or picking your foot up early.

Technique 5: Foot Placement

During brisk walking, each foot should be placed one to two inches to the side of an imaginary center line on the ground. Your feet and knees should be pointing straight ahead. This will help you walk in a straight line. When walking with weights or on rough terrain, you may need to use a wider foot placement.

As you bring your leg forward during the recovery phase, try to pull your leg straight forward. Your knee should pass beneath your hip joint. Your recovery leg should neither brush against your support leg nor swing out to the side.

Activity 8e

The purpose of this activity is to practice proper foot placement for fitness walking.

Read technique number five: foot placement. Have a partner observe first from the front and then from the back as you walk along a straight line. As you walk, place each foot parallel to and about one or two inches to the side of the line.

Technique 6: Arm Swing

During fitness walking, your arms should be bent at about a 90-degree angle at the elbow joint. Your hands should be in a relaxed fist position with your palms facing inward. From this position, your arms should swing forward and backward from the shoulder joint. Each arm should swing in a straight path and remain fairly close to your body to avoid side-to-side swaying of the upper body and hips. On the forward swing, your hand should rise at least to shoulder level. On the backswing, your elbow should rise as high as comfort will allow.

The arms play an important role in fitness walking. Your arms and legs are like teammates—the faster you swing your arms, the faster your legs will move.

Technique 6: Arm swing.

Activity 8f

The purpose of this activity is to focus your attention on your arm swing while fitness walking.

Read technique number six: arm swing. Using proper posture and alignment, practice the arm swing in a standing position. Start slowly and gradually increase the speed of your arms.

Ask a partner to check to make sure your arm swing is correct.

Technique 7: Breathing

Your breathing usually takes place without conscious voluntary control. It automatically adjusts to your need for oxygen. You can regulate your breathing to a certain degree by assuming conscious control of the depth and rate. However, if your breathing changes too much from the norm, your body will take over automatic control again.

If you start slowly and progress gradually, your breathing pattern will develop naturally, along with your other walking techniques. Breathing should not require thought on your part.

Even though your breathing will automatically adjust to your need for oxygen, it is generally more comfortable if your breathing is coordinated with your arm and leg movements. There is no set pattern that is right for everyone, and there is no one pattern that is right for every walking speed. Experiment with different speeds and breathing patterns until you find the ones most comfortable for you.

Activity 8g

The purpose of this activity is to help you start thinking about rhythmic breathing.

Read technique number seven: breathing. Begin walking at a slow pace. Try breathing in for three steps and out for three steps. Gradually increase your pace. At a faster walking pace, try breathing in for two steps and out for two steps.

Be aware of your breathing. It should be rhythmic and comfortable, but don't try to control it too much. Your body will automatically regulate the depth and rate of your breathing to meet your oxygen demand.

Technique 8: Hip Movement

To increase your walking speed, you must increase the length of your stride. One way to increase stride length is to turn your hips and allow them to add to your leg movements. By allowing your hips to turn, your back leg can go farther back and your forward leg can go farther forward.

Keep your back foot in contact with the ground until you have fully extended your leg and you push off from your toes. When swinging your leg to the front,

(a)   (b)

Technique 7: (a) Incorrect and (b) correct hip movement.

reach forward with your front foot as far as comfort will allow. This technique alone can add as much as eight inches to your stride length.

When you use your hips more, you reduce the amount of up-and-down movement in each step, and you convert wasted vertical energy into useful horizontal energy. Also, when you increase hip movement, you exercise the abdominal and hip muscles more vigorously.

Activity 8h

The purpose of this activity is to increase your stride length.

Read technique number eight: hip movement. From the ready position, take one giant step forward, extending your right leg as far forward as it will comfortably go. Hold this position for three seconds, then lift your right foot and move it another three to five inches forward. Hold this new position for ten seconds. Return to the ready position and repeat the procedure with your left leg. Perform this activity five times with each leg.

Have a partner measure your normal walking stride from the heel of your forward foot to the toes of your back foot. Then measure your stride after allowing your hips to follow through. Remember to keep your foot in contact with the ground as long as possible. Now compare the measurements to discover the distance added to your stride length when you include hip movement.

Technique 9: Leg vault.

Technique 9: Leg Vault

Incorporating the leg vault into your walking movement will add even more forward drive to your push off. For this technique it is helpful to think of your support leg as a vaulting pole. Heel contact is the pole plant of fitness walking. Swing one leg forward. At the point of contact, your leg should be straight, but not rigidly locked into extension at the knee joint. The idea is to reach out with the front leg and make contact with the ground using the longest practical stride. But do not drive your heel into the ground with a stiff leg.

Vault your body forward using your support leg as a vaulting pole. Your leg should be straight throughout the heel-to-toe roll and the push off. Finish the vaulting action with your leg extended, finally pushing off from your toes.

Activity 8i

The purpose of this activity is to familiarize yourself with the feeling of straightening your support leg.

Read technique number nine: leg vault. Practice the "robot walk," keeping your legs straight and using the heel-to-toe roll. Do not bend the knee. In this exaggerated activity, you will be able to notice how each legs acts like a vaulting pole.

Next, start walking in slow motion and stop just before you finish the push-off technique. Ask a partner to check to make sure your push-off leg is straight. Walk at progressively faster speeds as your partner watches your push-off leg. Make sure there is no bend at the knee joint until the leg starts to swing forward during the recovery phase.

Technique 10: Racewalk

This advanced technique requires accelerated arm and leg speed. In this technique you walk as fast as you possibly can. To walk faster, you must swing your arms and legs faster, so this is an extremely tiring technique. You need to gradually build up your time and distance using this all-out speed.

Racewalking is not for beginners, it is for intermediate and advanced fitness walkers who want a higher-intensity workout. High-intensity racewalking could result in very sore muscles, or even injury, for unconditioned beginners.

Activity 8j

The purpose of this activity is to learn how to add speed to your fitness walking. This technique is especially important if you plan to increase the intensity of your workouts.

Technique 10: The racewalk.

Read technique number ten: the racewalk. After you have warmed up properly and have walked for several minutes, begin moving your arms and legs faster as you walk. Begin by racewalking for short distances. Recover by walking at a slower pace between these sprints. Gradually increase the distance you can racewalk as you increase your cardiovascular endurance and leg strength.

Next, count the number of racewalk steps you can take in one minute. An easy way to determine your steps-per-minute is to count how many steps you take with your right foot in one minute and multiply by two. This is much easier than trying to count every step when you are walking at very fast speeds. The maximum effective leg speed you will probably be able to achieve with a four-foot stride is about 200 steps-per-minute. For most fitness walking workouts, a range of 130 to 180 steps-per-minute is good.

Fitness walking, like other sports and fitness activities, requires good technique for optimal performance. By focusing on one technique at a time and practicing regularly, you will soon become a highly skilled fitness walker.

Tips for Higher-Intensity Workouts

Once you have mastered the basic fitness walking techniques and have developed your cardiovascular fitness to a high level, you may find it difficult to reach your training heart rate. Here are some ideas to help you increase the intensity of your fitness walking workouts once you have reached this advanced level of training. High-intensity workouts should not be used by unconditioned beginners.

Vigorous Arm Swings

Begin with your elbows bent at a ninety-degree angle, your fists relaxed, and your palms facing inward. Swing your arms in a straight path, forward and backward, keeping your arms close to your body. Swing your arms higher, then pump your arms more vigorously and add movement at the elbow joint. On the upswing pull your forearm toward your upper arm and on the downswing push your forearm back down to a ninety-degree angle at the elbow joint. You may even want to tighten and relax your fist with each arm swing.

The additional muscle contractions of your arms will increase your oxygen demand. The increased oxygen demand will cause your oxygen delivery system to work harder and result in a higher-intensity workout.

Vigorous arm swings.

Hill Walking

Hill walking increases your exercise intensity and adds variety to your walking routine. It will also improve your cardiovascular fitness level. Depending on the steepness of the hill, your heart rate will increase ten to fifty beats per minute when walking uphill. This increase in your exercise heart rate makes hill walking an excellent cardiovascular conditioner and a great calorie burner.

Stair Walking

Stair walking is a superb exercise for your cardiovascular system. In addition to the aerobic benefits, stair walking develops muscular strength in your legs and hips since you must lift your body weight with each step. To increase your exercise intensity and to add variety to your fitness walking program, try stair walking.

Weights

An advanced fitness walker may wish to add hand or wrist weights to increase exercise intensity. When using hand and wrist weights, your arm swing should be controlled. Hand weights should not make you feel unbalanced. Start off with one pound weights and gradually increase as your conditioning improves.

Beginners are advised not to use weights as they start their walking program.

How many ways can you think of to increase the intensity of a fitness walk? Which, if any of these, are appropriate for your present level of fitness?

Fitness Walking Techniques

1. Posture and alignment
2. Heel contact
3. Heel-to-toe roll
4. Push off
5. Foot placement
6. Arm swing
7. Breathing
8. Hip movement
9. Leg vault
10. Racewalk

Weight Loss

9

Although no one wants it, millions have it—too much body fat. Americans consume more fat and sugar than any other people in the world. As a result of this high fat and sugar intake, and a lack of regular exercise, there are 60 to 70 million adults and 10 to 12 million school-age children in the United States who are too fat.

How Much Is Too Much?

Many people use height and weight charts to determine what they should weigh. However, height and weight charts generally represent population averages, not ideal body weights. As the population becomes fatter, the averages on height and weight charts increase.

A second problem with height and weight charts is that being overweight is not a health problem as long as the extra weight is lean body tissue, or muscle. Therefore, it is quite possible for a muscular individual to be overweight, but healthy. It is not being *overweight* but *overfat* that causes health problems.

A third problem concerns normal-weight and underweight individuals. Although these people are considered to be within or below their normal weight range, they may have too much body fat to be healthy. Height and weight charts do not take into account levels of body fat.

A height and weight chart can provide you with some information about how you compare to population averages. It can also give you a general idea about whether or not you have accumulated too much body weight. Medical professionals often define obesity as being 20 percent above ideal weight. However, this method is not as accurate as measuring percent body fat.

What is percent body fat? It is the percentage of total body weight that is stored body fat. It is the amount of body fat, and not body weight, that is most important to your health. Thus, knowing your percent body fat is more important than knowing your weight.

Being overfat simply means that your body is composed of too much fat. Obesity refers to a condition in which an excessive amount of body fat has been stored. There is not enough accurate data to determine the exact level at which stored body fat becomes a serious health problem. However, experts generally seem to agree that men who are over 25 percent body fat and women who are over 30 percent body fat should be considered obese. (See table 9.1 for standards of percent body fat.)

Table 9.1   Percent Body Fat Chart.

	Men	Women
Too Much	More than 25 percent	More than 30 percent
Just Right	10–15 percent	15–20 percent
Too Little	Less than 5 percent	Less than 10 percent

Why Control Body Fat?

In the United States there are many physical, social, and psychological problems associated with having too much body fat. At other times and in other cultures, being overfat was a social advantage—a sign of prosperity and health. This is not true in America today. Thin is in. The fashion world contends that to be attractive, people must be slim. Some Americans are obsessed with being thin. But more important than fashion concerns are health concerns related to having too much fat.

There are many reasons for not allowing yourself to become obese. Obesity is associated with several heart disease risk factors including high blood pressure, high cholesterol, and diabetes. Other health problems are also related to obesity. Strokes or kidney problems may result from high blood pressure. Blindness, heart attacks, strokes, and fat-clogged arteries can occur in an obese individual with diabetes. Obesity has also been associated with certain cancers such as breast cancer for women and prostate and colon cancer for men. The obese may also suffer from degenerative joint diseases such as arthritis.

Along with these serious illnesses, obesity has been linked to a shorter life span. Some research indicates that those who are moderately overfat may have a 40 percent higher than normal risk of a shortened life span. Obesity may result in a 70 percent higher than normal risk of a shortened life span.

In America, there are also social stigmas attached to being fat. The overfat are viewed as unattractive, inadequate, unhealthy, undisciplined, insecure, depressed, having poor personalities, having higher anxiety levels, and having lower self-concepts than normal-weight people. These characteristics are certainly not true of everyone who is overfat. However, those who carry too much fat are still perceived this way by some people.

As a result of social conditioning, the overfat often encounter teasing, ridicule, and rejection. In turn, psychological problems may result in a poor body image, a sense of failure, a passive approach to life situations, and an expectation of rejection.

What Causes the Overfat Condition?

The most common cause of obesity is taking in more calories than you use up. The human body is very good at storing these excess calories in the form of body fat. In the United States, most people have access to an abundance of food. Meanwhile, modern technology has developed many new labor-saving devices. The net result is that the physical effort of daily life has decreased while the availability of food has increased. For millions of Americans, this has led to the accumulation of too much body fat.

Until recently, obesity was thought to be caused by overeating. However, recent evidence suggests that lack of exercise is more often the culprit. The overfat do not necessarily eat more than their normal-weight counterparts—they are often less active.

In a few rare cases, glandular malfunction or some other medical problem may be the cause of obesity. However, for the vast majority of Americans, the problem is that they take in more calories than they use on a regular basis.

Obesity does not occur overnight. *Creeping obesity* is a term referring to the gradual accumulation of stored body fat. For the average American, a gradual decrease in physical activity begins in the late teens or early twenties. During this decline, eating habits tend to remain constant. It is not hard to see that if you continue to take in the same number of calories, but use less of them, the excess will be stored as body fat. As a result of this pattern, the average adult American gains about one pound a year. This doesn't sound like an alarming amount of weight until you figure that by age fifty, you will have accumulated about 30 pounds of excess body fat.

Along with the decrease in calorie use that occurs with a decrease in activity, there is also a gradual loss of muscle tissue. Less muscle tissue combined with the gradual accumulation of stored body fat results in a rather rapid change in percent body fat. In addition, resting metabolic rate (the number of calories needed at rest) also decreases with age. This decrease may be related to the loss of muscle tissue due to inactivity or it may be a natural occurrence during the aging process. At any rate, if you maintain your eating habits and decrease your level of physical activity as you age, you are almost certain to accumulate excess body fat.

This problem is not limited to adults. If children take in more calories than they use up on a regular basis they also become obese. A very high percentage of obese children and adolescents become obese adults.

How Can You Measure Body Fat?

Although body fat cannot be measured with absolute accuracy, there are several methods of estimating body fat that have proven to be fairly reliable and accurate. Methods for estimating percent body fat include: underwater weighing, measuring water displacement, X ray, ultrasound, electrical impedence, measuring body girth, and skinfold measurement. Of these, skinfold measurement is one of the least expensive, most accurate, and most available methods.

About 50 percent of body fat is stored just beneath the skin. Skinfold calipers can be used to measure the thickness of a fold of skin and the fat directly under it. When measurements are taken at specific body sites, the thickness of the skinfolds can be used to obtain an estimate of total body fat.

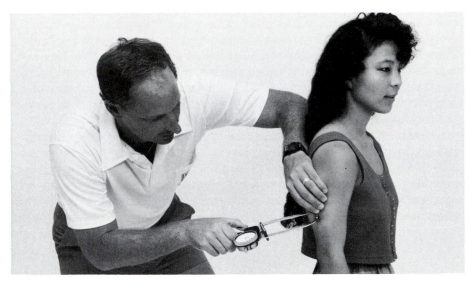

Using skinfold calipers to measure triceps skinfold.

Activity 9a

The purpose of this activity is to estimate your percent body fat using skinfold caliper measurements.

Guidelines for Making Skinfold Measurements

1. All of the skinfold measurements should be made on the right side of the body.
2. The skinfold should be picked up between the thumb and index finger.
3. Measure the thickness of the skinfold approximately one centimeter from the fingers and at a depth that is equal to the thickness of the fold.
4. Make three measurements at each skinfold site. Use the average of the three measurements as the skinfold thickness for that site.
5. Release and regrasp the skinfold for each measurement.
6. Measurements made by two different people may vary slightly. If you are measured a second time, have the measurements made by the same person at the same time of day.

Skinfold Sites

To determine percent body fat for women, use the sum of the skinfold measurements at the tricep, iliac crest, and thigh.

To determine percent body fat for men use the sum of the skinfold measurements at the chest, abdomen, and thigh.

Triceps Skinfold—Locate a point on the back of the upper arm halfway between the top of the shoulder and the tip of the elbow. Measure a vertical skinfold.

Iliac Crest—Locate a point on the side of the waist above the crest of the hip bone and slightly toward the front of the body, where there is a natural diagonal skinfold.

Thigh—Locate a point on the front of the thigh halfway between the hip joint and the knee joint. Measure a vertical skinfold.

Chest—Locate a diagonal fold halfway between the front of the armpit and the man's nipple.

Abdomen—Locate a point one inch to the right of the umbilicus and measure a vertical skinfold.

Use of the Nomogram

Add your three skinfold measurements (in mm) and mark this sum on the appropriate line of the nomogram. Place your age on the nomogram. Use a straight edge to connect these two points. Mark the place where the straight edge crosses the correct percent body fat line for your sex. What is your percent body fat?

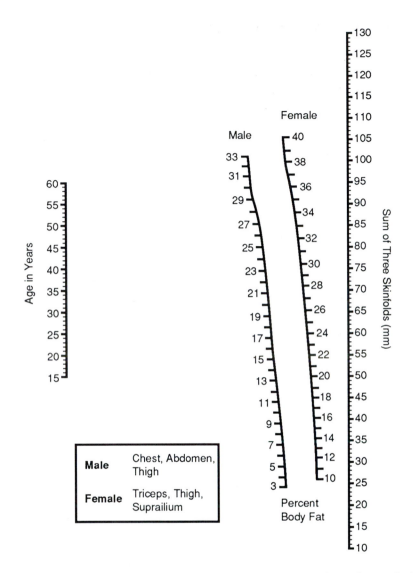

Baun, W.B., Baun, M.R., & Raven, P.B., 1981. A nomogram for the estimate of percent body fat from generalized equations. *Research Quarterly for Excercise and Sport.* 52:380 84

Nomogram.

What Can You Do About Body Fat?

The energy-balance equation states that for your weight to remain constant, you must use up as many calories as you take in. When the amounts are unbalanced, your weight changes. There are approximately 3,500 calories in one pound of stored body fat. If you take in an extra 500 calories a day without increasing your energy output, you will gain about one pound of body fat every seven days. Of course, the opposite is also true. If you take in 500 calories per day less than you use, you will lose about one pound every seven days.

The healthiest and most effective way to lose body fat is to combine a well-balanced diet with regular, moderate exercise.

A well-balanced diet is your source of dynamic energy. It should consist of nutritiously prepared foods high in nutrients. Your diet must provide all of the calories necessary to meet your energy needs. It must also include all of the nutrients necessary for healthy body maintenance. If essential nutrients are missing, your body cannot continue to function properly.

Exercise helps use up calories. Since muscle contraction requires energy, the more your muscles contract, the more calories you use. Experts agree that exercise plays a key role in reducing the loss of lean body weight (muscle) and promoting fat loss. When you diet, as much as half of your weight loss can be from protein and muscle. You want to lose fat, not muscle. Moreover, the failure rate of dieting by itself is high. Therefore, exercise should be included in a weight management program.

Why is it inadvisable to rely on diet alone to accomplish weight loss?

Fitness Walking and Weight Loss

Fitness walking makes five major contributions to your weight management program: it increases caloric expenditure, controls appetite, helps maintain resting metabolic rate, uses fat while increasing muscle mass, and helps reduce stress and tension.

Fitness walking uses up a lot of calories. Like other aerobic activities, it uses the large muscle groups of your body in repeated contractions for a relatively long period of time. Fitness walking for a mile uses about the same number of calories as jogging a mile. Walking just takes longer. See table 9.2 to discover how many calories you can use based on your walking pace and body weight.

Table 9.2   The Caloric Cost of Walking (calories/mile).*

Walking Pace (mph)	Body Weight				
	100 lbs.	125 lbs.	150 lbs.	175 lbs.	200 lbs.
			Calories Burned		
3.0	52	66	79	92	105
3.5	54	67	80	94	107
4.0	58	72	87	101	116
4.5	65	81	97	113	129

*Based on Bubb, et al. 1985. *Journal of Cardiac Rehabilitation* 5:462–65.

Fitness walking should not increase your appetite. Studies of humans and animals have indicated that exercise of light to moderate intensity and duration does not increase appetite, and may even reduce it.

Fitness walking may help keep your resting metabolic rate up while dieting. It increases the number of calories you use as you walk, and keeps your metabolic rate elevated after your workout is finished. Thus, your body continues to burn calories at a faster pace for several hours afterward. You use up more calories than you normally would at rest. An elevated metabolic rate also makes you feel more alert and alive.

Fitness walking builds fat-burning cells (muscle) while it reduces the size of fat-storing cells. Based upon the research to date, it appears that you cannot reduce the actual number of fat cells in your body. However, you can shrink their size and reduce the percentage of your body weight that is stored body fat. Since fitness walking is not as exhausting as some other forms of exercise, it is possible to exercise longer and burn more total calories.

Finally, fitness walking helps reduce stress and tension. The temptation to cheat on a diet is greatest during times of stress and tension. After a stressful, unpleasant day it is common to seek a pleasant experience. Many people find pleasure in eating and drinking. Going for a walk removes idle snacking time and helps reduce stress and tension.

Tips for Weight Control

If weight control is more important to you than cardiovascular health, you might adjust your fitness walking program by decreasing the intensity, increasing the duration, and increasing the frequency of your workouts. This could result in the expenditure of more total calories during exercise. However, it is recommended that you stick with the exercise guidelines for fitness walking programs listed in chapter 7. By following the guidelines, you can expect three major benefits from your fitness walking program: cardiovascular fitness, weight control, and stress reduction.

One of the keys to permanent weight loss and fat reduction is to take weight off slowly. Gradually reducing excess body fat allows you to remain healthy and motivated. Develop a new, healthier lifestyle that you can maintain for the rest of your life.

If you try to remove excess body fat too quickly, you are more likely to experience illness or injury. When this occurs, you will have to stop your program until you are well again.

Losing weight too quickly may also result in the "yo-yo syndrome." This is a cycle of losing weight and then regaining it. If the weight is lost quickly, by diet alone, as much as half of the weight loss can be lean body tissue or muscle, while the weight that is regained is mostly fat. The more often weight is lost and regained, the more fat is accumulated. This cycle can also lead to a unique form of high blood pressure called dieter's hypertension.

You should not attempt to lose more than one or two pounds of fat per week. To lose one pound of fat per week, you will need to create a caloric deficit of 500 calories a day adding up to 3500 calories a week. If you fitness walk two and a half miles, you will burn about 250 extra calories. If you give up one hamburger, you will take in about 250 calories less. Neither of these should be extremely difficult. You need not starve yourself on a diet or totally exhaust yourself with exercise if you combine diet and exercise.

During the first six to eight weeks of your exercise program, you may not lose any weight. Because muscle is more dense than fat, you may actually experience a slight increase in body weight during this time. However, since the weight gained is muscle and the weight lost is fat, your body circumference measurements should decrease. Beginning exercisers will often lose inches while remaining at the same body weight.

If you believe you need to lose a considerable amount of weight, be smart and safe—check with your physician. Your doctor should be able to tell you if it is safe for you to combine a caloric reduction diet with a fitness walking program. Your physician may refer you to a dietician for an individualized diet plan.

Fad diets are frequently advertised in newspapers and magazines. Can you find at least three such ads that violate the principles of weight reduction described in the text?

Spot Reduction

A common misconception about exercise is that you can spot reduce. Spot reduction is losing fat from a specific body part by exercising that body part. Examples of spot-reduction techniques include doing sit-ups to remove fat from the abdominal area or side bends to lose fat from the side of your waist. Research indicates that spot reduction does not work.

So-called spot reduction exercises will develop the muscle tissue under the stored body fat and increase the strength or muscle endurance of the muscle tissue. However, unless a total caloric deficit is created in the body, it appears that none of the energy expended will be taken from stored body fat. Even if a caloric deficit exists in the body, there is no evidence that a muscle can obtain energy from the nearest body fat storage area.

Guidelines for Fat Loss

Diet

Well-Balanced Diet

Food Groups	Recommended Daily Servings
Grain products	4
Fruits and vegetables	4
Dairy products	2
Meat	2
Junk food	0

Amount

Maintain recommended daily servings.
Eat smaller servings.
Not below 1,200 daily calories (women).
Not below 1,500 daily calories (men).

Exercise

Type	—Aerobic
Intensity	—60–90% of maximum heart rate
Duration	—30–60 minutes per session
Frequency	—5–7 days per week

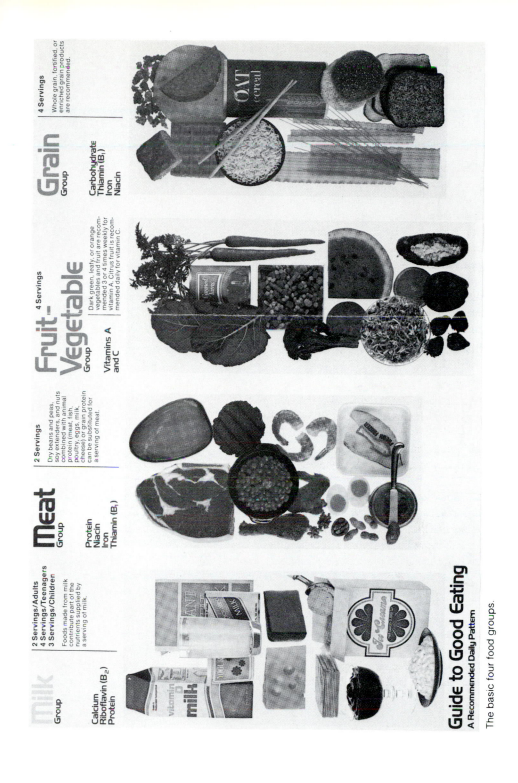

milk
Group

Calcium
Riboflavin (B₂)
Protein

2 Servings/Adults
4 Servings/Teenagers
3 Servings/Children

Foods made from milk
contribute part of the
nutrients supplied by
a serving of milk.

Meat
Group

Protein
Niacin
Iron
Thiamin (B₁)

2 Servings

Dry beans and peas,
soy extenders, and nuts
combined with animal
protein (meat, fish,
poultry, eggs, milk,
cheese) or grain protein
can be substituted for
a serving of meat.

**Fruit-
Vegetable**
Group

Vitamins A
and C

4 Servings

Dark green, leafy, or orange
vegetables and fruit are recommended 3 or 4 times weekly for
vitamin A. Citrus fruit is recommended daily for vitamin C.

Grain
Group

Carbohydrate
Thiamin (B₁)
Iron
Niacin

4 Servings

Whole grain, fortified, or
enriched grain products
are recommended.

Guide to Good Eating
A Recommended Daily Pattern

The basic four food groups.

Mental Benefits

10

Although most people are aware of the physical benefits of fitness walking, they may not be aware of the mental benefits. Many regular fitness walkers believe the mental benefits are just as important, if not more important, than the physical.

Your mind and body can only be separated in theory, for the purpose of study and discussion. In reality, the human body is one totally integrated organism that cannot be separated into component parts. Anything that affects your mind affects your body, and anything that affects your body affects your mind. An example of this mind-body relationship is a stomach ulcer that has resulted from constant worrying.

Stress Reduction

Your mental and physical health are affected by your ability to manage stress. Medical doctors have estimated that as much as 70 percent of all illness may be stress-related. Too much stress can lead to high blood pressure, heart disease, depression, schizophrenia, indigestion, increased cholesterol concentration, low back pain, headaches, cancer, and lower resistance to disease. Too little stress is also harmful. It can lead to boredom, loneliness, and even suicide.

Humans adapt best to moderate stress (eustress rather than distress). This is positive, enhancing stress that helps overcome laziness and provides the drive to produce and excell. Each individual has a relative stress level that is ideal for him or her. Your own moderate stress level should be located somewhere between being overbusy and being bored. This level creates a feeling of well-being that promotes optimal performance and efficiency.

College can be a time of great stress. College students are exposed to a variety of stressors that can make their college experience challenging. These stressors include time constraints, noisy and crowded conditions, fear of rejection and failure, pressure to conform, financial problems, career anxiety, and many others. Important decisions must be made during these years that can affect the rest of your life.

One healthy coping strategy for dealing with excess stress is regular exercise. Fitness walking helps release the muscular tension that accumulates when you are under stress by alternately and rhythmically contracting and relaxing your muscles. This action pumps fresh blood and oxygen to all the living cells of your body. It also carries away the accumulated chemical waste products of stressful muscular tension, leaving you with a refreshed, alert feeling.

Figure 10.1
The Stress Chart.

When you anticipate a stressful day, plan your fitness walk to follow the stress period. Then compare your tension levels prior to and following the walk.

Fitness walking provides an opportunity to take a mini-vacation from the pressures of everyday life. It can provide time to be by yourself or with others, depending upon which is most relaxing for you. Many regular walkers report that their fitness walking programs help them deal with relationships, expectations of others, money problems and other concerns. Fitness walking ranks high as a stress management technique and an excellent lifetime activity for relieving stress.

Positive Self-Esteem

The concept of self-esteem includes a feeling of personal worth, success, achievement, self-respect, and self-confidence. To build self-esteem, it is important to feel good about yourself in a specific area. This area should reflect your own interests, abilities, and opportunities. While some students excel in the classroom, others are successful in sports or music.

Success breeds success. The feelings you gain by satisfying your need for self-esteem are apt to encourage you in other achievements, which further builds self-esteem.

Many students drop out of college because of low self-esteem and a lack of confidence. People who suffer from low personal worth feel helpless and hopeless. They find it difficult to be successful.

A fitness walking program can help build self-esteem. It helps develop self-discipline, which can lead to a sense of accomplishment and a feeling of personal worth. Every fitness walking workout is a victory over laziness and low self-respect. The positive physical benefits that occur as a result of a regular walking program can also contribute to an increase in self-confidence.

Believe in yourself and your abilities. Recognize your limitations and expect to grow from them. People who feel good about themselves regard their own opinions and decisions as worthwhile.

Fitness walking, along with good nutrition and adequate rest, can help you accomplish your goals in school and in life. The more success you have, the stronger your self-esteem will be.

Improved Creativity and Problem-Solving Ability

A mental training program can be combined with your fitness walking program to help you become a creative thinker. This, in turn, can help you become a better problem solver. Fitness walking increases the oxygen supply to the brain. This can result in improved thinking, better memory, more intense concentration, and heightened clarity of thought.

Some experts believe you can train yourself to think more creatively and become a better problem solver. To begin with, change your perspective. Look at things from a different point of view or a different angle. If you normally walk the same course every day, try walking in the opposite direction or walking somewhere else. If you normally walk in the evening, try a walk in the morning. If it rains, try a walk in the rain. You may see things you have never seen before when you change direction or walk in different weather conditions.

Mental exercises like these, combined with your fitness walking program, can help you to overcome obstacles that block your imagination. By working your "imagination muscle" while you walk, you can add creativity and originality to your thinking.

Once you begin to see from another point of view, you will be able to find new solutions to old problems. More options become available. You may even learn to view your work, play, and relationships with others differently.

Relief of Anxiety and Depression

There is still considerable discussion about the antidepressant effects of exercise. The opportunity to set and achieve realistic goals is important for the anxious or depressed individual. Fitness walking provides an opportunity to set goals and achieve them.

Sticking with a walking program develops self-control. Once self-control is established in one area, it can be applied to other areas. Gaining self-control through fitness walking can be used to replace negative behaviors (such as smoking, overeating, and alcohol and drug abuse) which often contribute to anxiety and depression. Replacing negative behaviors with positive behaviors (such as fitness walking and good nutrition) can lead to a feeling of accomplishment and improved overall health.

Many mental health professionals now recommend walking for anxious or depressed clients. They encourage their clients to get outdoors, open their senses, and appreciate nature, instead of sitting at home feeling closed in, anxious, and depressed. Some mental health professionals even walk with their clients during therapy sessions. This seems to help clients "open up" and better deal with their concerns.

Depending on the severity of the anxiety or depression, fitness walking can help people move away from a constant internal focus on their own problems. As their physical health improves, many depressed people stop feeling sorry for themselves. They begin to count their blessings and recognize the good in their lives.

Two major steps in overcoming anxiety and minor depression are becoming more relaxed and feeling content. Many physicians believe that exercise is nature's best physical tranquilizer. A regular program of fitness walking can serve as one strategy to help relieve some types of emotional anxiety and control minor depression.

Increased Sense of Well-Being

A regular fitness walking program can increase the brain's supply of endorphins. Endorphins are naturally secreted hormones that act as the body's natural opiates. These morphinelike substances work in your brain to lower the sensation of pain and provide a sense of well-being. Research studies show that regular exercise increases the flow of endorphins to your brain and keeps them there longer. The moderate amount of endorphins released during fitness walking produces a feeling of being refreshed and energized. This leads to a positive exercise addiction. Those who exercise regularly say exercise makes them feel good, and they often don't feel quite right when they skip their exercise sessions.

Improved Sleeping Habits

Do you often lie awake at night with your mind racing, wishing you could fall asleep? Do you wake up in the morning feeling as if you haven't slept at all? A regular fitness walking program can contribute to a reduction in mental and physical tension. This can help you fall asleep more easily and sleep more soundly.

Better Quality of Life

A consistent and lifelong exercise program such as fitness walking increases your ability to enjoy your leisure time. In addition, your productivity at school and work should improve, leading to more hours of satisfaction. Having more energy and enthusiasm may also lead to new opportunities. Others will begin to notice the "glow" radiating from you when you are in excellent physical condition and optimal health. Feeling good about yourself, learning to enjoy every day, and improving the quality of your life may be the ultimate benefit of a fitness walking program.

Sticking with It

11

The most difficult part of an exercise program is sticking with it. Research and experience indicate that people need more than knowledge of the benefits or fear of negative consequences to stick with an exercise program.

Most adults in the United States know that a moderate amount of exercise on a regular basis would improve their health. Why then, do so many Americans still choose not to exercise? Some have even been advised by physicians to participate in a regular exercise program lest they prematurely die. Yet, many still choose not to exercise.

Rehabilitation exercise programs for heart attack survivors have reported that only about 50 percent of these individuals will stick with an exercise program. This high drop-out rate exists even though the heart attack victims realize an exercise program will reduce the risk of another heart attack. Clearly, neither knowledge nor fear is a strong enough motivator for exercise adherence.

Although walking has a better adherence rate than many other exercise programs, the drop-out range is still 25 to 50 percent. That means one or two people out of every four who begin a fitness walking program will quit. Will you quit? Or will you be one of the people who has what it takes to make a commitment and stick with your fitness walking program?

What is your health worth? Can you ever buy it back after you have lost it? Keeping healthy isn't just a matter of luck. Adopting and maintaining a regular exercise program is one way to invest in a lifetime of good health.

Motivation

The most important psychological obstacle to regular exercise is lack of motivation. Self-motivation is strongly related to sticking with your fitness walking program. One important question to ask yourself is whether you believe your daily activities have an impact on your health. If you answer yes, you are more likely to feel you have control over your own health.

Being healthy, physically fit, and attractive will help you gain more personal control over your life. Beginning a fitness walking program can be an important first step toward taking this control. People who demonstrate control over their lives tend to be happier. In fact, high-control people are twice as likely to say they are happy as low-control people.

Many people start exercise programs every year. Why do some stick with it while others drop out? One answer is motivation. Those who are highly motivated stick with their exercise programs. They don't allow any obstacles to interfere with their workouts. Those who are not highly motivated look for reasons to skip exercise sessions and drop out.

There are many motivational strategies that have proven successful for exercise adherence. What works for one person may not work for another. If you are highly motivated to exercise for your health, you may find several strategies that work well for you.

Motivational Strategies

Set Clear and Definite Goals

Establishing goals gives you direction. What do you want to achieve as a result of participating in a fitness walking program? If the goal is something you highly desire, you can become motivated to achieve it.

To be effective, your goals must be realistic. An unrealistic goal is to lose 100 pounds of body fat in two weeks. Although there are many factors to consider, the bottom line is that a realistic goal should be attainable. A realistic goal might be to lose 1 to 2 pounds a week by participating in regular fitness walking and reducing caloric intake.

Set goals you believe you can achieve. When you achieve a goal, you can always set another one. Since success breeds success, each time you achieve a goal you gain confidence in yourself and your ability to achieve the next goal.

To achieve a goal it must be measurable and clearly defined. "I want to get in good shape" is a noble desire but not very specific goal. How will you know when you are "in shape?" A good goal might be "I will be able to walk briskly for two miles by (a specific date)." When you walk on that day, you will know whether you have accomplished your goal. If you have, set another definite goal. If you have not, evaluate your exercise program and make the necessary adjustments.

An important step in the goal-setting process is writing your goals down. Written goals are much more powerful than unwritten ones and much less likely to be changed. By writing your goals down, you become more committed to achieving them. They also provide clear outcomes to strive for and a way to measure your progress.

Activity 11a

The purpose of this activity is to fill out a fitness walking contract that will reaffirm your commitment to reach the goals you have set for yourself.

Once you have clearly defined your goals, fill in the contract below.

I, _____ , commit myself to improving my health by following a fitness walking program.

The specific health and fitness goals of my walking program are:

1.
2.
3.
4.
5.

The specific date(s) I expect to reach my goal(s) are:
Other important reasons why I have committed myself to a fitness walking program:

1.
2.
3.

Guidelines to follow that will help me stay with my fitness walking program:

1.
2.
3.

Support people that will help me with my fitness walking program:

1.
2.
3.

When I reach my goals, I will reward myself by:
If I fall short of my goals, I will punish myself by:

Signature _____ Date _____

Witness_____ Witness _____

Reward Yourself

Reward yourself when you reach one of your goals. Give yourself something special—something you really want. Of course, it should be a healthy reward such as a small vacation, new walking shoes, new clothes, a new music tape, or just a pat on the back. Only you can decide on an appropriate reward for yourself.

For some people, it is difficult to look too far into the future. These people want the instant gratification or daily rewards after each workout. Before and during the exercise session, these secondary rewards can provide an incentive to walk. Looking forward to this special treat may be motivation enough to complete the walk. Examples include: taking a refreshing shower, watching a favorite television show, or going out for the evening.

Maintain a Positive Attitude

Often the difference between success and failure is attitude. A positive attitude produces positive results. You can program your mind for success by believing in yourself. With a positive attitude, you will look forward to each exercise session and enjoy your fitness walking program. Each workout can provide another opportunity to have fun and improve your health.

Strive to maintain a positive attitude every day you walk. Enjoy each walk. Think pleasant thoughts. It takes at least twenty-one days for a new behavior to become a habit, so the first month of your fitness walking program is critical.

If you allow your attitude toward fitness walking to become negative, or if it becomes something you feel you have to do instead of something you want to do, you might be headed toward failure.

Fitness walking should become an important part of your regular schedule, just like eating and sleeping. Don't ever wonder *if* you will walk today, know *when* you will walk today. Build it into your regular schedule. Once you begin to experience the beneficial effects, fitness walking will become its own reward because it will make you feel much better.

Close your eyes and imagine yourself achieving your goals. Make use of this self-fulfilling prophecy. If you repeatedly focus on some vision of yourself, it becomes part of your identity and you feel obligated to live up to it. Write your own script for who you want to be and how you want to live. Tell yourself over and over, "I will stick to my exercise program." This will soon become a part of you and you *will* be more likely to stick to your walking program. Fitness walking provides a great opportunity to repeat positive affirmations while you do something healthy.

Make Fitness Walking a Priority

Once you decide to include fitness walking in your life, make a commitment. Place a high priority on your fitness walking time. Don't allow anything to interfere with your scheduled exercise time.

Regularity is important to the success of an exercise program. Regular exercise will soon become a healthy habit, as brushing your teeth, eating well-balanced meals, and sleeping an adequate amount of time are.

If you do not place a high priority on your fitness walking time, you might be setting yourself up for failure. If you decide to exercise whenever you have time, you'll frequently find that you don't have time. Irregular exercise is not very beneficial and can be harmful. An unplanned, irregular exercise program may soon deteriorate into no exercise program at all.

Take responsibility for your health and life. Be in charge. If you value your health, place a high priority on good health habits. To reach your goals, you will need to put forth your best effort. Reaching worthwhile goals will require dedication, discipline, and persistence.

Activity 11b

The purpose of this activity is to help you set priorities and identify the things that are most important to you.

List the ten most important things in your life right now. After you have written them down, rank them from one to ten. Is your health or your appearance in the top ten? If one of them is, and it is one of your primary reasons for exercising, you are more likely to stick with your fitness walking program. If your health and your appearance are not important, you are more likely to be an infrequent walker and eventually a fitness-walking dropout.

Create a Personal Balance Sheet

This motivational strategy involves weighing the advantages and disadvantages of participating in a fitness walking program. The advantages of fitness walking are listed in chapters 2, 9, 10, and 12. Whenever you are tempted to skip a walk, look at the lists of advantages. This will provide you with extra incentive to put on your fitness walking clothes and take the hardest step of all—the first one.

Activity 11c

The purpose of this activity is to create a personal balance sheet to weigh the advantages and disadvantages of participating in a fitness walking program.

Draw a vertical line down the center of a blank sheet of paper. At the top of the left side of the page write the word "Advantages." At the top of the right side of the page write the word "Disadvantages." On the left side of the paper list all of the benefits and advantages to be gained by regular participation in a fitness walking program. Refer to chapters 2, 9, 10, and 12 if you need help remembering the advantages. When you have listed all the advantages and benefits you can think of, turn to the right side of the paper and list the disadvantages of participating in a fitness walking program.

Post this list where you will see it every day. This may provide additional motivation to continue your fitness walking program.

Plan

Many people are so busy doing, they don't have time to plan. Consequently, a great deal of their time is not spent wisely. Every individual has exactly twenty-four hours to spend each day. What you should spend your time on depends upon what you want. How well you spend your time depends not only on how well you plan, but also on how well you follow your plan.

Good habits are vital to success. Planning is a good habit. Plan a daily schedule, write it down, and follow it. Be sure to include fitness walking in your daily plan—set aside time for walking.

Do It

One of the most common barriers to success is procrastination, or putting things off. Instead of starting a fitness walking program next year, next month, next week, or tomorrow, start today. Do it now. Change to a healthier lifestyle right away.

Chart Your Progress

Keep a regular exercise log. Record each fitness walking session. This will provide an account of your progress. The visual feedback will give you motivation and a sense of accomplishment, which may well help you stick with your fitness walking program.

There are many ways to chart your progress. Find the type of recordkeeping that is right for you. Some people like to put a check mark on a chart or a calendar. Others like to keep detailed records of the exact distance they walk, the exact amount of time they spend, the exact exercise heart rate they maintain, and so on.

Date	Pulse	Minutes	Miles	Comments

Figure 11.1
One example of a progress chart.

Walking with others can provide motivation.

Charting your performance allows you to see your progress and determine how close you are to reaching your goals. It is rewarding to see the positive changes that take place as a result of regular fitness walking.

Walk with Others

Walking with others is a strong motivator. It turns fitness walking into a social activity, which can make it more enjoyable. Walking with others provides you with companionship and encouragement. You are more likely to stick with your fitness walking program when you know that someone is counting on you to be at a designated meeting place at a designated time.

Add Variety

Boredom is sometimes an excuse for quitting an exercise program. While following the same routine every day appeals to some people, others are easily bored with repetition. Variety is the answer. If you become bored with repetition, use your creativity to invent new ways of adding variety to your fitness walking program.

Explore new routes (parks, golf courses, hiking trails, beaches, new neighborhoods, and so on), find new exercise partners, use earphones to listen to the radio or tapes (be careful around traffic), walk backwards, use different walking speeds, walk in the shallow end of a swimming pool or in the ocean, use hand weights, walk hills, walk stairs, walk to complete errands, park farther away, or enter walking events. These are only a few ideas. Invent other variations for your fitness walking program. Be alert to signs of burnout and change your routine before it's too late.

Motivation tends to drop off during extreme weather. Alternatives during hot weather include walking when it is cooler—in the early morning or late evening. Alternatives during cold or wet weather include walking in malls, in indoor recreational facilities, and up and down stairwells.

Select a Pleasing Route

Safety should be your first consideration when you select a place to walk. Traffic must always be taken into account. There are areas in some cities that are never safe at any hour. Choose the safest and most attractive route that is available to you. Some suggestions are parks, country roads, safe neighborhoods, and golf courses.

Cross Train

Cross training involves the use of other fitness activities to replace or supplement your fitness walking program. Participating in other fitness activities can help you prevent burnout by increasing variety. Cross training can also help you stay active and produce more complete development.

With fitness walking as your primary exercise, you may choose to add other activities such as swimming, rowing, cross-country skiing, aerobic dancing, weight training, biking, tennis, racquetball, basketball, or jogging. Combining these activities will increase your cardiovascular fitness. In addition, they can help you develop muscular strength, muscular endurance, healthy body composition, and flexibility. You'll most likely receive a motivational boost from this variety, which will inspire you to maintain consistent fitness workouts.

Reduce Barriers to Exercise

Staying on a regular fitness walking program means not giving in to convenient excuses such as "I'm too tired," "It's too cold to walk," "It's too hot to walk," "I don't have time to walk," "It's too dark to walk," and so forth.

The following tips are recommended for reducing some of the barriers to exercise:

1. Place your walking shoes by the door so you will not have to hunt for them.

2. Keep your walking clothes in the same convenient place so you can always find them quickly and easily.

3. Lay out your walking clothes the night before if you plan to walk in the morning. If you plan to walk later in the day, lay out your walking clothes in the morning to remind you.

4. Schedule your fitness walking early in the morning. Later in the day, your time to walk will be more likely to conflict with other activities, commitments, and priorities.

5. Use cue cards containing inspirational messages. Place them in strategic places, such as your bathroom mirror or your refrigerator door. The cue cards will assist you in programming your mind with positive statements. Examples of

inspirational messages include "I'm really looking forward to my walk today," "I'm going to look great when I lose ten pounds," and "It's going to feel wonderful to relieve the stress and tension."

Find out which motivational ideas work for you and use them to maintain your fitness walking habit.

Join a Club

Walking clubs are being formed throughout the United States. There may already be a walking club at your college or in your hometown. You may want to join an established walking club or form one of your own.

Walking clubs can offer classes to teach the benefits of fitness walking and guidelines for healthy walking programs. Members can help each other learn fitness walking techniques that improve performance. They can also provide support and encouragement for each other. A walking club could set up an awards program to recognize the achievements of its members.

During periods of extreme weather such as long, cold winters or hot summers, the club may be able to gain access to an indoor facility or build one of their own. They might even conduct fundraising projects for charities or arrange trips to special walking events.

Participate in Special Events

Organized walking events are becoming popular. These events offer distances for all fitness levels. Striding events are also being organized across the country. Instead of being competitive, these events are more like a parade.

In addition to the striding events, many 5-kilometer and 10-kilometer racewalking events are held annually. The number of racewalkers participating in these events is growing rapidly.

Setting challenging personal walking goals for yourself can provide additional motivation for your fitness walking program. For example, if you complete your first 5K in a time of forty-five minutes, you may decide to set a goal to complete your next 5K race in forty-three minutes. This may add more direction and meaning to each training session and keep you looking forward to participating in your fitness walking program.

Work for a Presidential Sports Award

A Presidential Sports Award is available for fitness walkers. The goal is to walk 125 miles in fifty days, which averages out to 2.5 miles a day. Once you are walking 3 miles a day, send off for the forms. When you complete all of the requirements, send the forms in and you will qualify for a patch, a medal, and a certificate. The address is

Presidential Sports Award
P. O. Box 706
Old Chelsie Station
New York, NY 10011

Evaluate and Modify

As the weeks, months, and years pass, changes will occur. Your needs, interests, fitness level, living conditions, weather, and the availability of exercise facilities will change. As these changes take place, you will need to periodically evaluate your fitness walking program to determine if it is still providing the correct amount of exercise. The key is to maintain a program that meets your current fitness needs and interests.

Motivational strategies play an important role in sticking with your fitness walking program. Experiment with different ideas and find those that work best for you. Refer back to this chapter whenever you need a dose of encouragement or a shot of motivation. Keep in mind the most important health and fitness benefits come from a regular, lifelong program.

Activity 11d

The purpose of this activity is to identify motivational strategies that will help you stick with your fitness walking program.

Place a check by all of the motivatational strategies you believe will help you stick with your fitness walking program. Once you have selected these strategies, try each one. Then incorporate the strategies that work the best for you.

_____ Set clear and definite goals
_____ Reward yourself
_____ Maintain a positive attitude
_____ Make fitness walking a priority
_____ Create a personal balance sheet
_____ Plan
_____ Do it
_____ Chart your progress
_____ Walk with others
_____ Include variety
_____ Select a pleasing route
_____ Use cross training
_____ Reduce barriers to exercise
_____ Join a club
_____ Participate in special events
_____ Try to earn a Presidential Sports Award
_____ Evaluate and modify

Healthy Life-style

12

Many Americans are discovering the value of living a healthy lifestyle. There has been a significant increase in the number of people who desire a better quality of life. This increase is partly due to the findings of recent scientific studies. Evidence now indicates that positive lifestyle choices can have a significant influence on health, quality of life, and general well-being.

Living a quality life means enjoying your life and developing yourself in all areas. Health is one area that greatly affects the quality of life. The better your health, the more likely you are to achieve your fullest potential in other areas of life, including family, school, work, and leisure time.

Wellness is a term that refers to overall physical health. A wellness-oriented lifestyle contributes to one's general well-being. Proponents of wellness believe that making healthy choices helps reduce disease risk factors and leads to better health. These wellness experts encourage people to become more actively involved in their own health by taking more personal responsibility.

The current health problems in the United States are quite different from those at the turn of the century. During the early 1900s, the leading causes of death were infectious diseases such as pneumonia, influenza, and tuberculosis. At the present time, the leading causes of death in the United States are heart disease, cancer, strokes, and accidents. These causes are not infectious and cannot be spread from person to person. They are related to negative lifestyle behaviors such as smoking, poor nutrition, lack of exercise, obesity, chemical dependency, drinking and driving, and excessive stress.

Health

Health is a dynamic quality; it changes constantly. Your health includes your overall level of functioning at a particular point in time. Optimal health indicates a high level of functioning and is often characterized by vitality, zest for life, and a sense of harmony with nature and humanity.

Although you may be in good health most of the time, no one's health is constant. Everyone's health is occasionally affected by a cold, the flu, allergies, or other health problems. However, maintaining a healthy lifestyle should keep these health problems, and their duration, to a minimum.

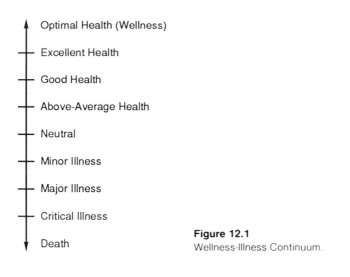

Figure 12.1
Wellness-Illness Continuum.

The Wellness-Disease Continuum

The Wellness-Illness Continuum shows that wellness, or optimal health, is the highest level of functioning possible. Optimal health is a condition in which all of the systems in your body are functioning perfectly. While this is the ideal to strive for, in reality, it can probably never be reached. It represents perfection, an uncommon human experience. The other end of the continuum represents the complete loss of functioning, or death. Every living person is somewhere between these two extremes. Where are you? Which direction is your lifestyle taking you? Are you headed toward a healthier and more abundant life, or toward suffering and premature death?

As you can see on the Wellness-Illness Continuum, absence of illness is not the equivalent of good health. Your position on the continuum is dependent upon your total health and is influenced by your degree of health in each of the following dimensions of life: physical, mental, emotional, social, environmental, psychological, spiritual, and vocational. The achievement of optimal health is related to the development of each of these areas.

Physical Health

Developing physical health includes working to become physically fit, eating a well-balanced diet with the recommended servings of nutritious foods, maintaining freedom from chemical dependency, and ensuring adequate sleep and rest.

Mental Health

Developing mental health include: continuing to expand your knowledge, sharing your knowledge with others, and increasing your creativity.

Emotional Health

Developing emotional health includes experiencing a variety of emotions but controlling your responses, expressing your emotions appropriately and comfortably, and showing respect and affection for others.

Social Health

Developing social health means building satisfying relationships with others and establishing a sense of belonging within your community.

Environmental Health

Developing environmental health means reducing environmental health hazards at home, on the job, and in your community. This includes avoiding or reducing your exposure to radiation, toxic wastes, air pollution, water pollution, noise pollution, and overcrowding.

Psychological Health

Developing psychological health means increasing your ability to deal with stress and to solve problems.

Spiritual Health

Developing spiritual health means believing in and accepting some unifying and controlling force more powerful than any one human being. It also means embracing and living according to a faith and value system that is consistent with your beliefs about that force. Spiritual health encourages living in harmony with your personal beliefs and values.

Vocational Health

Developing vocational health means seeking and finding job satisfaction and working in harmony with others to accomplish something worthwhile.

To achieve wellness, it is necessary to develop each of the eight dimensions of total health to some degree. Obviously, there should also be some balance to this development. A moderate degree of health in all eight dimensions is more desirable than extreme strength in some and extreme weakness in others. Each area can contribute to your health and your enjoyment of life.

Activity 12a

The purpose of the Total Health Wheel activity is to assess your current level of health in each of the eight dimensions.

On each line of the Total Health Wheel, place a dot that represents your current development in that area. Dots placed close to the inner circle (hub) represent a lower level of health, while dots placed near the outer circle (rim)

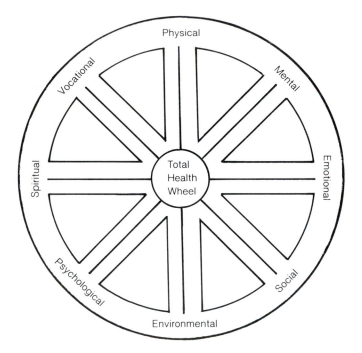

Total Health Wheel.

indicate a higher level of health. Connect the dots. How balanced is your development? Are you close to achieving a high level of health in each dimension? What are your strengths? What are your weaknesses? What behaviors can you adopt, modify, or eliminate to improve your health?

One key in your effort to achieve optimal health is to stay in touch with your feelings, attitudes, beliefs, and values. Only you can decide what combination of development in each dimension will make your life healthier and more enjoyable. Accept personal responsibility for your health. Improve your shortcomings while maintaining or further developing your strengths.

Major Factors That Affect Your Health

Your total health depends on many factors. Some of these factors are under your direct control; others are not. An awareness of the factors that are not under your direct control may help you deal more effectively with them. This is true even though you cannot directly control them. All of the factors are interrelated. They all influence each other, as well as your total health.

Major factors that influence your health include: lifestyle behaviors, inherited biological characteristics, your physical environment, social environment, psychological environment, medical care, accidents, injuries, and diseases.

Of all the major factors, lifestyle is currently the most important, and the one over which you have the most control. The choices you make today will lead to good health or illness later. The effects of these daily decisions are compounded over time—day by day, week by week, month by month, and year by year. The accumulation of good choices will move you toward optimal health and a quality life. The accumulation of bad choices will lead toward suffering, disease, and premature death.

Making wise choices and adopting positive lifestyle habits will enhance your health. If your lifestyle includes certain specific behaviors, your risk of disease will be lower and you may even live longer in good health. The following seven health practices were found to be highly correlated to good health.

1. Abstaining from the use of tobacco, especially cigarettes
2. Abstaining from alcohol, or drinking only in moderation (no more than two drinks per day)
3. Eating breakfast every day
4. Refraining from snacking between meals
5. Maintaining a healthy body weight and a healthy level of body fat
6. Sleeping seven to eight hours each night
7. Engaging in a moderate amount of exercise on a regular basis

Fitness Walking and a Healthy Life-style

Fitness walking is one behavior that can contribute to a healthy lifestyle. It is not a cure-all: it cannot solve all of your health problems. For you to develop to your full health potential and enjoy the benefits of a healthy lifestyle, fitness walking should be incorporated as one part of a much larger total health program. This larger program involves being aware of all the daily practices that have an impact on your health and modifying them in positive directions.

One place to start is by reducing your risk of cardiovascular disease, the number one cause of death in the United States. Lower your risk of cardiovascular disease by following these recommendations: stop smoking, exercise regularly, eat a healthy diet, control your blood pressure, and maintain a healthy body fat level.

Along with making changes, schedule a regular physical examination and regular dental examinations, practice regular self-examinations for breast cancer or testicular cancer, watch for signs of skin cancer, and follow safe sex practices. Also, practice relaxation strategies to reduce harmful stress, avoid smoke-filled environments, wear your seat belt every time you ride in a motor vehicle, and don't drink and drive.

Congratulations are in order if you have started a fitness walking program. You have taken a first step toward improving your health. You should not attempt to make too many changes in your lifestyle at one time. Change is uncomfortable. If you try to make too many changes, and you become too uncomfortable, you are more likely to revert back to your old, comfortable habits. This occurs even if you know your old habits are not good for you. Stick with your fitness walking program until it becomes a regular habit.

Enjoy your walk through life.

Once fitness walking becomes an integral part of your life, choose another health behavior to improve. As the years go by, maintain your strengths and work on your weaknesses. Since optimal health or wellness is an ideal that can probably never be reached, there is always room for growth and improvement. Continue to walk toward better health. And remember to enjoy the journey every day on your walk through life.

Activity 12b

The purpose of this activity is help you identify lifestyle behaviors that are enhancing or harming your health.

Place a check in either the positive or the negative column for each lifestyle behavior. Add up the positive behaviors and the negative behaviors. Are you satisfied with the results? What are your healthy lifestyle behaviors? What are your unhealthy lifestyle behaviors? What are your plans to improve the lifestyle behaviors that are detracting from your health?

Lifestyle Behavior	+	−
Abstain from tobacco use	_____	_____
Avoid smoke-filled environments	_____	_____
Abstain from alcohol consumption	_____	_____
Maintain a healthy body weight	_____	_____
Maintain a healthy percent body fat	_____	_____
Control your blood pressure	_____	_____
Get adequate sleep and rest	_____	_____
Engage in regular, moderate exercise	_____	_____

Lifestyle Behavior	+	−
Practice stress-management techniques	⎯⎯	⎯⎯
Eat breakfast daily	⎯⎯	⎯⎯
Maintain a well-balanced diet	⎯⎯	⎯⎯
Limit salt intake	⎯⎯	⎯⎯
Limit sugar intake	⎯⎯	⎯⎯
Limit fat intake	⎯⎯	⎯⎯
Wear seat belts	⎯⎯	⎯⎯
Avoid drinking and driving	⎯⎯	⎯⎯
Schedule regular physical examinations	⎯⎯	⎯⎯
Schedule regular dental examinations	⎯⎯	⎯⎯
Perform monthly self-exams for lumps or thickening of the skin	⎯⎯	⎯⎯
Practice safe sex	⎯⎯	⎯⎯
Maintain a positive attitude toward life	⎯⎯	⎯⎯
Abstain from the use of drugs	⎯⎯	⎯⎯

References and Suggestions for Further Reading

Allsen, P. E. 1978. *Conditioning and physical fitness: Current answers to relevant questions.* Dubuque, Ia.: Wm. C. Brown.

Allsen, P. E., Harrison, J. M., and Vance, B. 1984. *Fitness for life: An individualized approach.* 3rd ed. Dubuque, Ia.: Wm. C. Brown.

Alter, M. J. 1988. *Science of stretching.* Champaign, Ill: Human Kinetics.

Althoff, S. A., Svoboda, M., and Girdano, D. A. 1988. *Choices in health and fitness for life.* Scottsdale, Ariz.: Gorsuch Scarisbrick.

Anderson, B. 1980. *Stretching.* Bolinas, Calif.: Shelter.

Bowerman, W. J., and Harris, W. E. 1967. *Jogging.* New York: Grosset & Dunlap.

Brooks, G. A., and Fahey, T. D. 1985. *Exercise physiology: Human bioenergetics and its applications.* New York: Macmillan.

Brooks, G. A., and Fahey, T. D. 1987. *Fundamentals of human performance.* New York: Macmillan.

Brown, H. L. 1986. *Lifetime fitness.* Scottsdale, Ariz.: Gorsuch Scarisbrick.

Cairns, M. 1985. Racewalking—A fitness alternative. *Journal of Physical Education, Recreation, and Dance* 50–51.

Campbell, K. R., Andres, R., Greer, N. L., Hintermeister, R., and Rippe, J. 1987. The effects of fatigue on selected biomechanical parameters in fitness walking. *Medicine and Science in Sports and Exercise* 19: 518.

Coleman, R. J., Wilkie, S., Viscio, L., O'Hanley, S., Porcari, J., Kline, G., Keller, B., Hsieh, S., Freedson, P. S., and Rippe, J. 1987. Validation of a one-mile test for estimating VO2 max in 20–29 year olds. *Medicine and Science in Sports and Exercise* 19: 528.

Cooper, K. H. 1968. *Aerobics.* New York: Bantam.

Cooper, K. H. 1970. *The new aerobics.* New York: Bantam.

Cooper, K. H. 1977. *The aerobics way.* New York: Bantam.

Cooper, K. H. 1982. *The aerobics program for total well-being: Exercise, diet, emotional balance.* New York: Bantam.

Cooper, M., and Cooper, K. H. 1972. *Aerobics for women.* New York: Bantam.

Corbin, C. B., and Lindsey, R. 1988. *Concepts of physical fitness with laboratories.* 6th ed. Dubuque, Ia.: Wm. C. Brown.

Corbin, D. E. 1988. *Jogging.* Glenview, Ill.: Scott, Foresman and Company.

Couey, R. B. 1982. *Building God's temple.* Minneapolis: Burgess.

DeBenedette, V. 1988. Keeping pace with the many forms of walking. *The Physician and Sportsmedicine* 16(8):145–50.

deVries, H. A. 1986. *Physiology of exercise: For physical education and athletics.* 4th ed. Dubuque, Ia.: Wm. C. Brown.

DiGennaro, J. 1983. *The new fitness: Exercise for everybody.* Englewood, Colo.: Morton.

Dishman, R. K., ed. 1988. *Exercise adherence: Its impact on public health.* Champaign, Ill.: Human Kinetics.

Fixx, J. F. 1977. *The complete book of running.* New York: Random House.

Fox, E. L. (1984). *Sports physiology.* 2nd ed. Philadelphia: Saunders.

Fox, E. L., Bowers, R. W., and Foss, M. L. 1988. *The physiological basis of physical education and athletics.* 4th ed. Philadelphia: Saunders.

Fox, E. L., and Mathews, D. K. 1981. *The physiological basis of physical education and athletics.* 3rd ed. Philadelphia: Saunders.

Getchell, B. 1983. *Physical fitness: A way of life*. 3rd ed. New York: John Wiley & Sons.

Greer, N., Campbell, K., Andres, R., Hintermeister, R., and Rippe, J. 1987. An evaluation of walking and running shoes during walking. *Medicine and Science in Sports and Exercise* 19:517.

Greer, N. L., Campbell, K. R., Foley, P. M., Andres, R. O., and Rippe, J. M. 1986. An assessment of the reliability of ground reaction forces during walking. *Medicine and Science in Sports and Exercise* 18:S81.

Hagerman, G. R., Atkins, J. W., McMurtry, J. G., and Steadman, J. R. 1987. *Efficiency walking and jogging*. New York: Bantam.

Henderson, J. 1988. *Total fitness: Training for life*. Dubuque, Ia.: Wm. C. Brown.

Hesson, J. L. 1985. *Weight training for life*. Englewood, Colo.: Morton.

Hockey, R. V. 1985. *Physical fitness: The pathway to healthful living*. 5th ed. St. Louis: Times Mirror/Mosby.

Hoeger, W. W. K. 1986. *Lifetime physical fitness and wellness: A personalized program*. Englewood, Colo.: Morton.

Hoeger, W. W. K. 1988. *Principles and laboratories for physical fitness and wellness*. Englewood, Colo.: Morton.

Jonas, S., and Radetsky, P. 1988. *PaceWalking: The balanced way to aerobic health*. New York: Crown.

Kahnert, J. H. 1981. *Excellence in physical fitness*. 2nd ed. Dubuque, Ia.: Kendall/Hunt.

Kashiwa, A., and Rippe, J. 1987. *Fitness walking for women*. New York: Putnam.

Kline, G., Porcari, J., Freedson, P., Ward, A., Ross, J., Wilkie, S., and Rippe, J. 1987. Does aerobic capacity affect the validity of the 1 mile walk VO2 max prediction? *Medicine and Science in Sports and Exercise* 19:528.

Kline, G., Porcari, J., Hintermeister, R., Freedson, P., McCarron, R., Rippe, J., Ross, J., Ward, A., and Gurry, M. 1986. Prediction of VO2 max from a one-mile track walk. *Medicine and Science in Sports and Exercise* 18:S35.

Kline, G. M., Porcari, J. P., Hintermeister, R., Freedson, P. S., Ward, A., McCarron, R. F., Ross, J., and Rippe, J. M. 1987. Prediction of VO2 max from a one-mile track walk. *Medicine and Science in Sports and Exercise* 19:253.

Koszuta, L. E. 1988. Splash on by. *The Walking Magazine* August/September: 65–70.

Kuntzleman, C. T., and Editors of *Consumer Guide*. 1978. *The complete book of walking*. New York: Simon and Schuster.

Kusinitz, I., and Fine, M. 1987. *Your guide to getting fit*. Palo Alto, Calif.: Mayfield.

Lamb, D. R. 1984. *Physiology of exercise: Responses and adaptations*. 2nd ed. New York: Macmillan.

Levy, M. R., Dignan, M., and Shirreffs, J. H. 1988. *Essentials of life and health*. 5th ed. New York: Random House.

Makalous. S. L., Arauj, M. A., and Thomas, T. R. 1988. Energy expenditure during walking with hand weights. *The Physician and Sportsmedicine* 16(4):139–48.

Mazzeo, K. S. 1985. *A commitment to fitness*. Englewood, Colo.: Morton.

McArdle, W. D., Katch, F. I., and Katch, V. L. 1986. *Exercise physiology: Energy, nutrition, and human performance*. 2nd ed. Philadelphia: Lea & Febiger.

McCarron, R., Kline, G., Freedson, P., Ward, A., and Rippe, J. 1986. Fast walking is an adequate aerobic stimulus for high fit males. *Medicine and Science in Sports and Exercise* 18:S21.

McGlynn, G. 1987. *Dynamics of fitness: A practical approach*. Dubuque, Ia.: Wm. C. Brown.

Melograno, V. J., and Klinzing, J. E. 1988. *An orientation to total fitness*. 4th ed. Dubuque, Ia.: Kendall/Hunt.

Miller, D. K., and Allen, T. E. 1986. *Fitness: A lifetime commitment*. 3rd ed. Edina, Minn.: Burgess.

Montoye, H. J., Christian, J. L., Nagle, F. J., and Levin, S. M. 1988. *Living fit*. Menlo Park, Calif.: Benjamin/Cummings.

Noble, B. J. 1986. *Physiology of exercise and sport*. St. Louis: Times Mirror/Mosby.

O'Hanley, S., Ward, A., Zwiren, L., McCarron, R., Ross, J., and Rippe, J. M. 1987. Validation of a one-mile walk test in 70–79 year olds. *Medicine and Science in Sports and Exercise* 19:528.

Porcari, J., Kline, G., Hintermeister, R., Freedson, P., Ward, A., Gurry, M., Ross, J., McCarron, R., and Rippe, J. 1986. Is fast walking an adequate aerobic training stimulus? *Medicine and Science in Sports and Exercise* 18:S81.

Porcari, J., McCarron, R., Kline, G., Freedson, P., Ward, A., Ross, J., and Rippe, J. 1987. Is fast walking an adequate aerobic training stimulus in 30–69 year old adults? *The Physician and Sports Medicine* 15:119.

Prentice, W. E., and Bucher, C. A. 1988. *Fitness for college and life.* 2nd ed. St. Louis: Times Mirror/Mosby.

Rippe, J., Ross, J., Gurry, M., Hitzhusen, J., and Freedson, P. 1985. Cardiovascular effects of walking. *Proceedings of the Second International Conference of Physical Activity, Aging, and Sports,* p. 47.

Rippe, J., Ross, J., McCarron, R., Porcari, J., Kline, G., Ward, A., Gurry, M., and Freedson, P. 1986. One-mile walk time norms for healthy adults. *Medicine and Science in Sports and Exercise* 18:S21.

Rippe, J. M., Ward, A., and Freedson, P. 1988. Walking for health and fitness. *Encyclopedia Brittanica Medical and Health Annual.*

Ross, J., Gurry, M., Ward, A., Walcott, G., Hitzhusen, J., and Rippe, J. 1986. Accuracy of predicted max heart rate in the elderly. *Medicine and Science in Sports and Exercise* 18:S95.

Schwartz, L. 1987. *Heavyhands walking.* Emmaus, Pennsylvania: Rodale.

Stokes, R., and Faris, D. D. 1983. *Fitness for everyone.* Winston-Salem, N.C.: Hunter.

Stokes, R., Moore, A. C., and Moore, C. 1986. *Fitness: The new wave.* 2nd ed. Winston-Salem, N.C.: Hunter.

Stutman, F. A., and Africano, L. 1985. *The doctor's walking book.* New York: Ballantine.

Sweetgall, R., Rippe, J., and Katch, F. 1985. *Rockport's fitness walking.* New York: Putnam.

Sweetgall, R., and Dignam, J. 1986. *The walker's journal.* Newark, Delaware: Creative Walking.

Terry, J. W., Johnson, D. J., and Erickson, C. R. 1984. *Physical activity for all ages: Concepts of high-level wellness.* 2nd ed. Dubuque, Ia.: Kendall/Hunt.

Thaxton, N. A. 1988. *Pathways to fitness: Foundations, motivation, applications.* New York: Harper & Row.

Vitale, F. 1973. *Individualized fitness programs.* Englewood Cliffs, N.J.: Prentice-Hall.

Walcott, G., Coleman, R., MacVeigh, M., Ross, J., Gurry, M., Ward, A., Kline, G., and Rippe, J. 1986. Heart rate and VO2 max response to weighted walking. *Medicine and Science in Sports and Exercise* 18:S28.

Walking for fitness, a round table. 1986. *The Physician and Sportsmedicine,* 14(10):145–49.

Ward, A., Wilkie, S., O'Hanley, S., Trask, C., Kallmes, D., Kleinerman, J., Crawford, B., Freedson, P., and Rippe, J. 1987. Estimation of VO2 max in overweight females. *Medicine and Science in Sports and Exercise* 19:528.

Weinberg, R., Caldwell, P., Cornelius, W., Jackson, A., and Smith, J. 1982. *Health-related fitness: Theory and practice.* Topeka, KS: Jostens.

Wilkie, S., O'Hanley, S., Ward, A., Zwiren, L., Freedson, P., Crawford, B., Kleinerman, J., and Rippe, J. 1987. Estimation of VO2 max from a one-mile walk test using recovery heart rate. *Medicine and Science in Sports and Exercise* 19:528.

Williams, M. H. 1985. *Lifetime physical fitness: A personal choice.* Dubuque, Ia.: Wm. C. Brown.

Wilmore, J. H., and Costill, D. L. 1988. *Training for sport and activity: The physiological basis of the conditioning process.* 3rd ed. Dubuque, Ia.: Wm. C. Brown.

Yanker, G. 1985. *Gary Yanker's walking workouts.* New York: Warner.

Yanker, G. 1983. *The complete book of exercisewalking.* Chicago: Contemporary.

Zwiren, L. D., Freedson, P. S., Ward, A., Wilkie, S., and Rippe, J. 1987. Prediction of VO2 max: Comparison of five submaximal tests. *Medicine and Science in Sports and Exercise* 19:564.

Index

Stress
    and aerobic exercise benefits, 11
    chart, 96
    reduction, 95–97
Stretching, 43–47
Suggestions for further reading, 119–21
Sunglasses, 26
Surfaces, walking, 37
Sweetgall, Robert, 5–6
Swimming, 9

Target zone, 69
Techniques, fitness walking, 71–82
Test
    fitness walking, 49–56
    re-. *See* Retesting
Thigh, skinfold, 87
Tobacco, 115
Total health wheel, 113–14
Training
    cross, 108
    over-. *See* Overtraining
Triceps, skinfold, 87

University of Massachusetts Medical School,
    50, 57
Upper shoe, 21

Variety, 107–8
Vocational health, 113–14

Walkers and Talkers, The, 2
Walking
    and aerobic exercise, 8–11
    and American Heart Association, 68–69
    and clothing, 19–28
    clubs, 2, 109

    and elderly and handicapped, 5
    and equipment, 19–28
    and exercise, 17
    hill. *See* Hill walking
    mall. *See* Mall walking
    night. *See* Night walking
    organized events, 2, 109
    and priority, 104–5
    programs, 57–70
    race-. *See* Racewalk
    and safety, 29–30
    shoes. *See* Shoes
    and sports, 15
    stair. *See* Stair walking
    surfaces, 37
    techniques, 71–82
    test, 49–56
    and weight loss, 16, 83–94
    See also Fitness walking
Walking Magazine, The, 2
Warm-up, 41–42, 69
Water aerobics, 9
Weather, extreme, 30–32
Weight, of shoe, 23
Weight control, tips, 90–91
Weight loss, 16, 83–94
Weights, 81–82
    fitness walking. *See* Fitness walking
    hand. *See* Hand weights
Wellness-illness continuum, 112–14
Wet weather, 32
Wheel. *See* Total health wheel
Workouts, high-intensity, 80–82

Yellow maintenance program, 65

Zone, target. *See* Target zone